WALKING TALL

OVERCOMING INNER SMALLNESS
No Matter What Size You Are

To Charles + Eco—
Love you guys Big Time.
Kup shining that bright light
+ walking Tall!
♡ Peg

WALKING TALL

OVERCOMING INNER SMALLNESS
No Matter What Size You Are

Peggy O'Neill

WALKING TALL

OVERCOMING INNER SMALLNESS

No Matter What Size You Are

Peggy O'Neill
Copyright 2002
Small Miracles Press
P.O. Box 269
Ojai, CA 93024

Printed in the United States of America
Library of Congress Control Number: 2001117937

ISBN: 0-9710170-0-X

Cover Design by Ben Cziller
Interior Book Design by Bren Frisch
Cover Photo by Rick Ransier

This book is
dedicated to my
parents who have
given me the gift
of life, and to my
teachers who have
given me the gift
of freedom.

ACKNOWLEDGEMENTS

I'd like to appreciate *every person* who has ever expressed belief in me because, without you, I would never have had the strength, perseverance, or faith to complete this book.

Thank you to Alice Kane who held my hand during the infancy of this project while it was trying to find its form. Thank you for always being kind, gentle, and true. Thank you to my editor Barbara McNichol for transforming chicken scratch into legible English, and for being so easy to work with. Thanks to Faye Heimerl for your fabulous proofing and discerning eye. Thanks to Bren Frisch who made this book so beautiful on the inside, and to Ben Cziller who designed a cover that rocks. Thanks to Rick Ransier for your long friendship and great photos. Thank you to all my pals who reviewed early stages of the book and gave astute and constructive feedback. Thank you to all my close friends during this process who continually pumped me with kudos and love. Thank you to Christine Testalini who gave me a map for self-publishing and guided me directly to my first publisher. Thank you to my publicists, the Visioneering Group. Let's sell some books, guys! Thanks to Marci Shimoff who first saw potential in me for being a speaker/author and for leading the way into this wonderful and exciting world. Thanks to all my famous buddies who so graciously endorsed this book and honored me.

Thank you, most of all, to my husband Brad Laise. Honey, your constant flow of love and adoration could make any fool think they could write a book. Thank you for taking care of everything when I was buried six feet under mounds of text, scads of layout details, and multiple rewrites. Thank you for all your encouragement— from eyes, smiles, words, and good humor—every time I was ready to throw it all in the trash. Thanks to our dogs Keesha and Wicki, too, for your quiet company through all these months, and for keeping my feet warm. Thanks to all the forces that gave me everything I needed to create this book. May it bring more light to the world.

TABLE OF CONTENTS

INTRODUCTION

I know of a woman who started her career as a news reporter. She progressed to a headline anchor position and eventually hosted her own talk show. The talk show was so successful, she won an Emmy Award for television excellence. When she was called on stage to receive her Emmy, the whole country cheered her on. She was thrilled; this was the pinnacle of her career so far.

She later reported underneath all the excitement, she also felt sad and embarrassed about being overweight. She admitted she could not take in the full joy of the moment because, inside, she felt unworthy.

This woman's name is Oprah Winfrey.

Oprah told this incredible story in her movie, "Make the Connection." This story illustrates that no matter how glorious the recognition we receive, if we don't feel good about ourselves, we can miss out on the splendor of life. Instead of experiencing joy and fulfillment, we feel empty and small inside.

Many people of gigantic social, political, or economic

stature feel small inside—afraid or inadequate for some reason. And their sense of inner smallness overrides everything that's happening on the outside. No matter how successful they might look to others, when inner smallness has a hold, they fail to experience what they came here for—happiness and peace—the birthright of us all.

As you can see, inner stature is of utmost importance. Stature happens to be something I know a lot about. It has been the thematic issue of my life. As an adult, I stand 3 feet 8 inches tall. That is, on the OUTside.

I came face to face with the devastating impact of inner smallness several years ago while living on a fruit farm in Hawaii with several close friends. I had creative, fulfilling work and earned a comfortable income. Everything on the OUTside was paradise. Yet, my inner anguish had escalated to such a degree that I didn't want to live any more.

At that point, I was plagued by my sense of inner smallness, which had compounded over time. I suppose it all began with my parents' struggle about having a child who looks different. It multiplied over the years, with kids throwing nasty names at me, boys being only interested in friendship, and employers closing their doors to me. Each experience of non-acceptance got piled on top of the past wounds of rejection and humiliation. I ended up getting a double dose of non-acceptance: small on the outside *and* small on the inside.

When my misery got so big that I didn't want to be here, I believed my outer smallness caused all my suffering. But the discovery of my life is this: *Outer stature does not dictate happiness; INNER stature does.*

My life has since been resurrected. My inner smallness has been transformed into inner BIGness. I now love my life and feel incredibly blessed to experience so much joy and love every single day. I am thrilled to have found a way to break free from all the torment, and to be so deeply nourished by the "little" things in life. I am so happy to be happy! I'm glad the resolutions I have made for myself can assist others. I delight in letting others know their outer situation doesn't matter much; what really matters is their INNER situation. What matters is knowing we have the power to increase our INNER stature. We can all be happy. We can all WALK TALL.

This book is about just that: how to break free from inner smallness and get BIG on the inside. It's about heightening your sense of courage and confidence. It's about developing the skills, habits, and character traits of a BIG person. It's about expanding your sense of compassion and contentment.

WALKING TALL teaches you to make healthy choices, take responsibility for yourself, overcome fear, and know the truth of who you are. By sharing stories about my own experiences, I hope to inspire you to celebrate your uniqueness, be powerful yet kind, and expand into your HUGE self!

The theme of this book is well stated in this famous quote by Marianne Williamson, which former South African President Nelson Mandela used in his 1994 Inaugural Speech.

Our deepest fear is not that we are inadequate. Our deepest fear is that we are powerful beyond measure. It is our light, not our darkness that most frightens us.

We ask ourselves, who am I to be brilliant, gorgeous, talented and fabulous? Actually, who are you not to be? You are a child of God.

Your playing small doesn't serve the world. There is nothing enlightening about shrinking so that other people won't feel insecure around you.

We were born to make manifest the glory of God that is within us. It's not just in some of us; it's in everyone.

And when we let our own light shine, we unconsciously give other people permission to do the same. As we are liberated from our own fear, our presence automatically liberates others.

-Marianne Williamson

So, read on and watch yourself get BIG inside! Enjoy the experience of WALKING TALL.

PART ONE

CHOICES

INTRO:
THE POWER
OF CHOICE

Though there are many things we cannot change, there are many *more* we can. That's because we have the power to choose.

Every day we make zillions of choices. We choose what we eat, when we sleep, and where we work. We choose our friends, associates and spouses, our clothing, our hair-styles, and the furnishings in our homes. We choose our interests, our level of commitment, how often we exercise, and what we do for fun.

> "
> *It is the ability to choose that makes us human.*
> "
> —MADELEINE L'ENGLE

Many people overlook the fact that we also choose what goes on inside our minds. We choose our thoughts, attitudes, and beliefs as well as the words we speak. Most importantly, we choose how we see ourselves and the world around us. Choices permeate our lives every day. They can either build us up or tear us down. This is the power of choice.

Making healthy choices means selecting what nourishes us and what will bring forth positive experiences, growth, and well-being. It means choosing thoughts, words, actions, and relationships that make our lives better.

Healthy choices are not always easy. Sometimes it's difficult to eat healthy while everyone around us eats junk food. Sometimes it's difficult to take time out for oneself when our family members have so many needs. Sometimes it's even difficult to choose having a healthy relationship with our "self" over continuing an unhealthy relationship with someone who brings us down.

Choosing what's healthy is not always easy, but in the long run, it can transform our lives.

Let's take a look at several areas where making healthy choices can have a powerful effect.

❶

HEALTHY
THOUGHTS

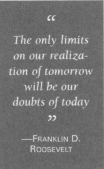

Perhaps the greatest power people possess is choosing their thoughts.

Thoughts are the foundation of human life—the basis of our attitudes, words, and actions. Our thoughts are the basis of what we say, what we do, and are expressed in the results of what we do.

So, our thoughts fundamentally influence our lives and well-being. Simply put, our thoughts can either cripple us, or allow us to WALK TALL.

Here's a story that illustrates the power of thoughts.

For my 16th birthday, my folks gave me a 35mm single lens reflex camera. I quickly became an avid photographer. For years, I carried that camera with me everywhere I went. I built a darkroom in the basement, had a summer photography business, and even won a few photo contests.

After ten years of pursuing my passion, I had a dream—to become a professional photographer! I was both thrilled and honored when I got accepted at the top commercial art school in America—Art Center College of Design in Pasadena, California.

At 17 with my trusty camera

I began my first semester with all engines roaring. I knew I was a talented amateur photographer and that I'd make an even better professional. Watch out world—here I come!

However, I was not really prepared for the severity of the task. During my first semesters, I worked about 80 hours a week. On top of that, I had an hour commute each way to school. On top of that, I no longer was shooting with a teenie tiny 35mm camera. UHH UHH! Now, I shot with a 4x5 field camera (about the size of a 25-inch television). I lugged that thing around with me everywhere, along with my 30-pound tripod, heavy metal stands, and lights that were bigger than my entire body. I quickly woke up to the fact that this was no party school!

Exhausted at the end of every semester, I wrestled with the idea of dropping out. Each time, my Art Center buddies would give me a big pep talk. "Once you have a diploma from Art Center, you're in-like-flint," they'd say to convince me. "You'll have no problem getting hired by ad agencies. That diploma is your ticket!" I knew what they said was the truth so I held tight to my dream, toughing it out through all eight semesters.

One month before my graduation, the dean called me into his office. I thought he wanted to critique my portfolio that I would soon be showing to ad agencies. When I sat down, he said, "Congratulations Peggy, on your upcoming graduation. You have accomplished a great deal." I was stoked! "But," he added, "I want you to know that when you go out in the real world, no one will hire you because of your size. I just want you to be warned."

His words must have resonated loudly with similar messages I had received earlier in life, because I believed him. His attack

Here I am toughing it out on the way to the darkroom.

continued to play over and over in my mind long after I left his office. I couldn't seem to shake it off. I guess I internalized his words, because I started telling myself, "I'll never get hired."

That voice continued running like a tape in my mind, over and over. And every time it did, I felt smaller and smaller on the inside. As a result, I never took the risk of showing my portfolio to any ad agencies. I never opened a photo studio. Instead, I gave up.

This is the power of thought.

SILENCE THAT CRITICAL VOICE

The dean's words weren't my biggest enemy; it was my choice to *internalize* his words. As a result, I started attacking myself. Not just once. I did it repeatedly! The repetition of that attack actually caused my doom. Outer attacks may hurt us. But inner attacks can devastate and destroy us.

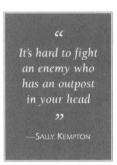

"
It's hard to fight an enemy who has an outpost in your head
"

—SALLY KEMPTON

We may not be able to control what other people say to us, but we certainly can control what we say to ourselves by defending against our inner critical voice, vigilantly and ruthlessly. If we don't defend against negative and demeaning thoughts, we can never really hope to WALK TALL.

Unfortunately, everyone has a critical voice inside

that can say cruel and nasty things. The extent of these attacks can be as big as life itself. The attacks may differ in nature, such as saying, "I could never do that," "I'm a loser," or maybe, "I'm not good (pretty, smart, strong, etc.) enough." But their outcome is always the same: inner smallness—lack of power, self-doubt, and self-sabotaging attitudes and behaviors.

That critical voice, the number-one cause of inner smallness, becomes our worst enemy.

To defend against inner attacks, we just need to silence them. We don't have to change our thoughts. We don't have to get into a discourse with our inner voice, arguing over whether we really are smart enough, or whatever enough. No inner argument; no need to implant positive thoughts. We simply have to silence that critical voice.

To do so requires *paying attention to our thoughts*. That means becoming conscious of the dialogue that goes on inside our minds while we walk, drive, groom, prepare a presentation, chat with a friend, and so on. This skill grows with practice.

How can you distinguish between when the voice inside supports you and when it beats you down?

Often the difference is difficult to discern because the words are similar. For example, the voice might say, "Next time work harder." Or it might say, "You never work hard enough." These similar phrases induce very different feelings. The first one prods you to grow and evolve; the second one puts you down psychologically.

You can tell the difference between the voices by the

feelings they evoke. When the internal voice makes you feel shameful, inadequate, less than, or just plain old bad, you can be certain you're hearing the critical voice. When it encourages you to do or be more, it is the voice of evolution. Silence that critical voice. Act in accordance with the encouraging, evolutionary voice.

So start paying attention to your thoughts as you go about your daily activities. Whenever you notice your current thought is negative, attacking, cruel and/or demeaning, practice defending. Do this by *firmly commanding that critical voice to STOP! or SHUT UP!* Here is an example:

> A while ago, I was quite nervous getting ready to give my first all-day seminar for a Fortune 500 company. Just moments before being introduced, I dashed down the hall to use the ladies room. As I started to bolt back to the meeting room, I faced a problem! The handle on the bathroom door was so high, I could just graze the bottom of it. And the door was so heavy, every time I managed to wedge it open just a bit, it would slip out of my fingers. Try as I might, on my tippiest of tippie-toes, I was trapped in the restroom! And late for my presentation!
>
> Now, I've been tardy a lot in my life and have been attacked for it on many occasions. Certainly, some of that criticism has stuck with me, and in this moment, my internal voice saw this as a perfect opportunity to

pounce.

"You'll be late— AGAIN! You irresponsible dweeb!"

Clearly criticism was **not** what I needed in this tense moment!

"STOP!" I said with command.

It stopped. Amazing! Then silence—providing space to seek a solution.

"What to do?" I looked around the bathroom for a stool or chair to hoist me up, but there was nothing. Hmm? What now? I began banging on the door.

My critical voice barged in again:

"They'll all think you're coo-coo for making such a racket."

Again, I told that voice to take a flying leap.

I continued banging louder and louder until someone finally heard me and set me free. I hopped onto the stage and began my talk on disabilities by sharing what had just happened. We all had a big chuckle; it became a perfect start for the day!

Silencing that critical voice made it possible for me to seek a solution, clear the obstacle at hand, and meet my next experience with both confidence and a smile. Silencing that critical voice allowed me to hop up on that stage WALKING TALL.

So, reflect for a moment. What are the words your critical voice beats you with? Maybe they have something to do with your body—maybe you're too heavy, too thin, too old, or too short. Maybe you criticize your-self for your personality. Maybe you didn't do well in school and you still badger yourself because you're not as quick as others. Maybe you have a bad temper or have had a string of bad relationships. Whatever it is, look and see. What are the exact words you hear? How do they make you feel?

Here's an exercise to help build your skill in silencing that critical voice.

EXERCISE   Spot and Stop

In your journal, make a list of the things your critical voice says to you *most* often. Whatever your inner critic puts you down for, write it here. Write in a stream of consciousness, not caring about grammar and punctuation. Just let your thoughts flow onto the paper. Make your list as long as you can.

When you think you have written everything, think again. Go deeper. List the criticisms you heard as a child and the names of people who used to say them to you. Underline or highlight the attacks that still come up even now as an adult. Read your list.

The more you bring to a conscious level the specific words, messages, and cruel attacks that hide in your subconscious or unconscious mind, the easier it will be to spot them so you can stop them. *Spot and stop.* Develop this skill and overcome the number-one cause of inner smallness. You can repeat this exercise as often as you wish.

EXERCISE   Pat on the Back

After you've been practicing silencing that critical voice for a week or so, make another list in your journal. This list will include the attacks you were successful at defending against during the past few days. When you've completed your list, read it over and pat yourself on the back. Keep up the good work.

Do this exercise once a week for two months, then as frequently as you wish. This will support you in becoming more conscious of the presence of your inner critic and its familiar themes. It's also good practice at recognizing your progress in learning a new skill and taking pride in it.

NURTURE AN ATMOSPHERE OF ACCEPTANCE

When you silence that critical voice inside, you begin to nurture an atmosphere of acceptance.

Acceptance is perhaps the greatest healing force that exists. Acceptance is the sister of love, maybe her mother. As we learn to accept ourselves, perfect or imperfect, we begin to embrace all of life and all of its wonders.

Nurturing an atmosphere of acceptance is one of the biggest steps you can take while learning to WALK TALL. Stop rejecting and ridiculing yourself. Then healing can take place. Then the well being unfolds and empowerment can grow.

DEFEND AGAINST OUTER ATTACKS

Let's look at how to defend ourselves against attacks from others.

Verbal attacks Unfortunately, we don't have much control over what others say to us. People of all sorts can say words that are downright nasty. Some parents and family members frequently point out our faults and criticize us. Some kids bully others. Teachers sometimes overemphasize our shortcomings. Strangers sometimes react to us unkindly. Regrettably, we live in world that can be cruel.

> "
> No one can
> make you feel
> inferior without
> your consent.
> "
>
> —ELEANOR ROOSEVELT

Verbal attacks come in various forms. They can be direct, such as "Homo!" or "You geek!" They can be indirect and sarcastic, such as "Aren't you the special one?" or "You haven't finished this *yet*?"

Verbal attacks put us down, criticize who we are, and doubt our capabilities. They paint us with shame. They let us know that we are *not* okay. They leave us feeling flawed, timid, and insecure. Even though verbal attacks can appear less offensive than physical attacks, many times their barbs go much deeper.

We can easily discern the degree of inner smallness or bigness people have by how they speak to others. Do they criticize and demean? Do they wash doom over the future? Do they embarrass us in front of others? Or do they provide hope and optimism? Do they encourage us to overcome obstacles? Do they keep sight of our fullest potential and guide us in that direction with loving-kindness?

When someone says something that insults, criticizes, or shames you, they are attacking you. To defend yourself, first you must *recognize the attack*, as you learned to do defending against your internal critical voice. Paying attention to your feelings and acknowledging to yourself when something offensive has been said will help you detect the attack.

Second, *defend yourself*. You can't exactly say, "Shut up!" But you can say something like, "You have no right to judge me" or "Your opinion doesn't matter." Communicate with diplomacy and directness.

In my case with the dean, had I been WALKING TALL at that time, I could have told him, "Sorry, I don't agree. Good day." or "You do not determine my future. I do." Then I would have walked out of his office.

By standing up for yourself, and speaking with firmness and strength, you let others know you aren't a pushover. Once they know you have the power to defend yourself, it's less likely they'll continue attacking you. Try it and see for yourself.

Depending on the nature of your relationship with the offender, you may choose a different third step. If the person badgering you is a stranger or acts in a hotheaded way, it might be best to just walk away. If, however, the tormentor is a person you encounter frequently at home, work, school, or wherever, you may find it helpful to have a dialogue. A dialogue can open the channels of communication, which will enhance your understanding of one another and may remedy the situation.

Attacks often occur when people are angry and/or are trying to communicate something important but don't know how to do so effectively. In either case, you can transform a bad relationship into a good one simply by having a conversation with the other person. People who WALK TALL work to gain understanding rather than trying to be right or prove their point.

The chart on the following page can guide you through transforming a fight into a friendship or a debate into a dialogue. This model was designed by Deborah Flick, Ph.D., and is discussed in detail in her book, *From Debate to Dialogue: Using the Understanding Process to Transform Our Conversations*. Have a look at the chart and see how the Understanding Process can transform your communication skills. You can use these tools for successful conversations with just about anybody.

A huge part of achieving success in any relationship —intimate, family or business—is being a good listener and a caring communicator. Approaching others with empathy and the desire to understand their experiences is the practice of a person with inner BIGness. Making the healthy choice to listen with openness to others can significantly increase the success of any relationship.

Folks with inner smallness are quick to attack, defend, and justify their position. They close themselves off to others. Their only interest is to "win" or get their way. They have a tiny perspective that does not extend beyond themselves. Their world consists only of "me, myself, and I."

	CONVENTIONAL DISCUSSION PROCESS	THE UNDERSTANDING PROCESS
PREMISE:	In any given situation there is one right answer or right perspective, usually one's own.	In any given situation there are multiple, valid answers and perspectives, including one's own.
GOAL:	To win, To be right, To sell, persuade or convince	To understand the other person from their point of view (To understand does not mean to agree)
ATTITUDE:	Evaluating and Critical	Curious and Open
FOCUS:	"What's wrong with this picture?"	"What's new? Of value? What can I learn?"
BEHAVIORS:	**LISTENING:** • Accept nothing at face value. • Hear advocacy as a challenge to be met. • Listen judgmentally. • Listen for errors and flaws. • Plan your rebuttal. • Talk more than you listen. **INQUIRING:** • Interrogate the other person. • Ask questions that: – Support your perspective. – Challenge other person's view. **ADVOCATING:** • Assert own position. • Describe flaws in other's perspectives. • Justify your position. • Defend your assumptions as truth.	**LISTENING:** • Accept what is said at face value as true for the giver. • Hear advocacy as an opportunity to deepen understanding. • Listen: – "For" their story. – Without judgement. • Listen more than you talk. • Reflect instead of react. **INQUIRING:** • Ask questions in order to: – Clarify and deepen your understanding. – Understand what another's ideas mean to him/her. • Explore taken-for-granted assumptions. **ADVOCATING:** • Offer your ideas as yours only. • Explore alternative points of view.
ROLE:	Devil's Advocate or Truth Sayer	Walk in Another's Shoes
OUTCOME:	**DEBATE**	**DIALOGUE**

It's not easy to set aside preferences, points of view, or desires to get your own way and remain open to another's point of view. That's why they say it takes a person of BIG character to do so.

Think of the last argument you had with a close friend or family member. Did you listen more than you spoke? Were you equally interested in understanding their experience as making your own point? Or did you ask questions to gather ammunition? Did you take a few deep breaths and remind yourself that winning is not important but coming to a mutual understanding is important? Did you form your words so they came across with respect and gentleness?

One practice that is extremely helpful in difficult conversations is active listening. In active listening, you repeat what your conversation partners say. This lets them know you understand what they are trying to communicate. This also lets them know their messages have been heard. Being heard and understanding others lead to openness, caring, and resolution.

The goal of active listening is effective communication, whether it's in a heated argument or an intense, decisive conversation. To communicate effectively requires hearing the thoughts, feelings, and concerns of one another. So use active listening to emphasize you understand what your partner has to say and ask for the same in return.

THE PROCESS OF ACTIVE LISTENING:

- Before either person says anything, both take a few deep breaths and let go of any tension in your bodies and emotions.
- Put on your listening cap, open your mind, and expand your sense of concern to embrace your partner in conversation.
- Choose which person will speak first and which person will listen first.
- The speaker begins talking about the issue at hand.
- The listener listens so carefully that s/he will be able to repeat what was said in a few moments.
- The listener repeats what s/he has heard, focusing on the speaker's main point. When s/he is able to repeat accurately what has just been said, switch roles and continue the conversation in like manner: one person speaking, the other repeating what has just been said.

If the listener cannot reiterate what the speaker has just said:
- Both parties take a deep breath.
- The speaker gently lets the listener know what aspect wasn't understood.
- The speaker then calmly makes his/her point again, saying it simpler and more succinctly, and asks for the repetition.
- When the listener repeats the point accurately, both switch roles.

There are varied styles of speaking. The speaker may talk calmly and pause after making each point to listen for the reiteration. Or the speaker can be quite "heated" emotionally and will have difficulty listening to the reiteration. When this happens, the listener interrupts the speaker and asks for a break so s/he can repeat the point back. This gives them both clarification that the intended point is being communicated.

GUIDELINES FOR THE SPEAKER:

- Speak in a calm voice.
- Express yourself clearly and with as few words as possible.
- Speak in "I" statements about how things make you feel rather than making "you" statements or accusations.
- Make one point, then pause and ask for the listener to repeat what you have just said.
- Listen carefully to what the listener is now saying.
- Be honest in your feedback: is what the listener just repeated accurate or not?

GUIDELINES FOR THE LISTENER:

- Sit up straight and look at your partner.
- Put all your attention into understanding what your partner is saying.
- If you cannot understand the point, ask the speaker to alter the manner of speaking (e.g., slow down, speak louder, etc.)

- Only interrupt the speaker if s/he has talked for a long time and you need to find out if you have heard the point correctly.

Throughout this process, remember to breathe, letting go of physical and emotional tension. Also remember your purpose is to understand one another. Be courteous, respectful, gentle, and kind.

This simple technique supports real communication. It helps build skills you can adapt to any conversation, whether you are repeating what your partner says or not. It helps strengthen your listening muscles, help you to expand outside of yourself, and allows you to let go of having to "win."

If you need to resolve a conflict with someone, try this listening technique and see how being heard can work magic on your relationship.

Physical Attacks Actions like shoving, punching, fighting, etc., are severe attacks and are considered highly offensive. You must report them to an authority immediately. To avoid being attacked physically, it's smart to stay away from folks who behave like this. It also helps to keep company with others; don't go walking down deserted streets alone.

Bullies pick on people they sense are weak and timid because they see the situation as an easy win. They do it to get a sense of "I'm on top!" This usually happens because they have been the target of someone's low self-esteem and abuse. And so the cycle continues—the under-dog trying to escape by being the top-dog.

You cannot "fix" bullies or their perpetrators. For that matter, you can't change anyone but yourself. So, if you don't want to get beat up or picked on, change. *Empower yourself physically.* Stand up straight. Speak with volume and certainty. Embody confidence. Work out. Learn to fight. Take a class on self-defense. Once you become powerful, you won't be an easy win. Bullies will respond to you differently when they find out you know how to kick butt, too.

HEALTHY ATTITUDE

Attitude is also a choice, an all important choice. A healthy attitude uplifts us, makes us strong, courageous, and able to persevere. An unhealthy attitude breeds defeat, magnifies doubt, drowns us in fear, and generates *lots* of inner smallness.

Let's look at some of the poignant

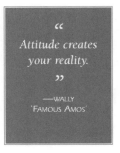

"
Attitude creates your reality.
"
—WALLY
'FAMOUS AMOS'

areas in which attitude can either make or break us.

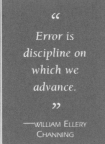

"
Error is discipline on which we advance.
"
—WILLIAM ELLERY
CHANNING

LEARN FROM YOUR MISTAKES

No matter if we are eight hours old or eighty years old, we are all learning. Nobody is born knowing how to do everything. Nobody is free from doubt when doing something new. Nobody is free of making mistakes. Indeed, nobody's perfect.

Yet some people have no mercy when it comes to mistakes. They seem to forget they are involved in an evolutionary learning process in all that they do. And when they falter, they have no ability to accept their mistakes. Instead of *using* the information they get out of the process, they ridicule themselves for not succeeding.

This type of attitude can only breed inner smallness.

We all began to walk by stepping, falling, and stepping again. What if a one-year-old fell while learning to walk and said, "Oh no, I failed! I can never learn to walk. I'm too embarrassed to let anyone see me fail again. I quit!" Although this example may bring a giggle, many people, young and old, respond with a similar attitude when dealing with their own shortcomings and mistakes.

You get to choose. You can either see your mistakes as a reason to put yourself down. Or you can look at your mistakes and see what you learned, then use each piece of information in your next attempt toward mastery.

Your attitude toward mistakes can deem you powerless and broken. Or it can provide valuable gifts in your evolutionary process. You choose.

STOP COMPARING

One of my best girlfriends in college had a lovely slim figure and a face so sweet, I had to smile when

I saw her. Her blatant beauty was also evident by her many suitors.

One curious thing about my friend—she bought lots of glamour magazines.

On budding spring days, we'd sit outside and soak up the warm sun with our shirt sleeves rolled up. As we did that, she would page through her beauty magazines. I'd notice her mood begin to sink. She'd say, "If only I looked like that! I'd be beautiful if only I was that thin."

> "
> How simple it is to love and how exhausting it is to find fault. For every time we see fault we think something needs to be done about it.
> "
>
> —MAHARISHI MAHESH YOGI

Comparing herself to magazine models whose images were probably air brushed to perfection could not be called a healthy habit. In comparing herself, my beautiful friend lost perspective on how attractive she was in the eyes of those around her. Her self-worth deflated as she dreamed to be someone else, while totally overlooking the magnificent gift she was embodying all the while.

I guess my friend is not the only one who participates in this rather bizarre form of entertainment, because here is a blurb I received through my e-mail not long ago:

"Did you know…If shop mannequins were real women, they'd be too thin to menstruate. There are 3 billion women who don't look like super-models and only eight who do. Marilyn Monroe wore a size 14. If Barbie was a real woman, she'd have to walk on all fours due to her proportions. The average American woman weighs 144 lbs. and wears between a size 12 and 14. One out of every four college-aged women has an eating disorder. The models in the magazines are air-brushed! They're not perfect! A psychological study in 1995 found that three minutes spent looking at models in a fashion magazine caused 70% of women to feel depressed, guilty, and shameful. Models who twenty years ago weighed 8% less than the average woman, today weigh 23% less."

—*Author Unknown*

Comparing ourselves to idols, whether they be known for their beauty, power, genius, or athletic ability, can be a sure ticket to the land of inner smallness. People with unhealthy attitudes see their idols in a magazine and say, "Look at how incredible *they* are. I could *never* be that awesome. If only I could be like them, *then* I would be happy." This type of comparing comes from a "small" mind and serves no one.

People who are BIG inside, or want to be big inside, see those who may be more beautiful, more powerful, or more talented than they are as a spark, a spark to ignite their own greatness.

They see their idols as an *inspiration*. In such a case,

they respond by saying something like, "One day, I want to be as great as him/her! I'm going to work every day to develop my strengths, so one day I, too, can enjoy such success and recognition!"

Every human being has his or her own magnificent attributes, strengths, and weaknesses. So, focus on the greatness of what you *do have*. Appreciate and express gratitude for even the smallest things. Work to become what you want to be. These are the habits that cultivate inner BIGness.

Stop comparing yourself to the model in the magazine and wishing you were someone else. Just be yourself! Celebrate your uniqueness!

Be the greatest "you" you can be, and always WALK TALL!

GET OFF THE PITY POT

Some people deal with life by whining and complaining. Others turn to blaming and shaming. Some people hope that if they sound helpless enough crying and whimpering they'll get some attention, and maybe even a hero will come along and save the day.

They sit on the pity pot. They are called victims.

Victims blame everyone else for their pain and misery and want someone else to fix their problems. They believe they are helpless and act accordingly. Victims do not take responsibility for themselves or for their lives. Every problem is someone else's fault. Victims rank the highest in inner smallness.

The pity pot and victimization are two attitudes with

the same flavor. Both fertilize inner smallness. Both disempower us. Both are cop-outs. I know this because sitting on the pity pot used to be one of my favorite pastimes.

> While I was growing up, I used the pity pot tactic to get attention from my mom who was often busy, and, later to connect with friends. One day, while on the path of getting BIG inside, I came to a crossroads. I had to choose between staying on the pity pot or WALKING TALL.

> I was afraid that if I got off the pity pot I wouldn't attract any friends. I was afraid if I quit complaining that I wouldn't have anything to talk about. So I took a chance. I decided to stop all that and see what I might attract from a new place.

> Amazingly, my relationships from that point on were totally different. They were based on people being attracted to what was true inside of me, instead of what was false. Consequently, they became interested because of my strengths instead of my weaknesses. They loved me not because of my need, but simply because of who I was.

If you want to WALK TALL, you must take responsibility for yourself, your situation, and your world. If you want to be happy, you have to BE happy. You have to take affirmative action to change what needs to be changed. You must rise up with courage and strength, clarity and conviction, and step forward.

Take the energy you spend on complaining, blaming and playing the victim and use it instead to take responsibility for yourself and create positive change.

The truth is you are magnificent and you are capable of great things. View life from that perspective and see what happens!

> **EXERCISE** Repeating Question:
> **What's right about being a victim?** For directions on how to do a "repeating question" please refer to the instructions in the exercise on page 233.

FIND THE GIFT INSIDE THE CHALLENGE

Every single person walking the face of the earth has difficulties and challenges to deal with. No matter what package, duration, or dosage they may have come in, we all have crosses to bear. This is the human condition.

Some folks have more challenges than others, with no logic or fairness to make sense of it. I don't think anyone understands it completely or necessarily likes the way it is.

Some of our challenges offer no options. We have no choice about where we come

> "
> Wounding opens the doors of our sensibilities to a larger reality. Pathos gives us eyes and ears to see and hear what our normal eyes and ears cannot.
> "
>
> —JEAN HOUSTON

from, who our parents are, our race, our disabilities, our height, or our illnesses. But we can choose the attitude with which we respond to these challenges. Our attitudes can either be life supporting or life damaging. Our attitudes can either fill us with inner smallness or support us in WALKING TALL.

Probably the biggest challenge I've met so far is that of being a Little Person. In every phase of my life, it has presented me with a new set of difficulties. As a child, I was teased and called nasty names almost daily. At school, I couldn't reach the water fountain or hang up my coat. On the playground, I was often one of the last chosen when picking teams. As an adolescent, I was excluded from romance and dating, and wasn't allowed to compete in team sports. As a young adult, potential employers saw my height before my talent. As a woman, my ability to be an adequate mother was doubted. Driving a car is impossible without adaptations. In my home, I must use stools and ladders to function. Through all of this, I despised my challenge and felt a prisoner to it.

I avoided my problems for a very long time, and over time, they just got worse. When they became life threatening, I sought professional help. I then started sorting through my challenges. As the process continued, something unexpected emerged. I came to see a **purpose** in all my difficulties. In truth, I wasn't cursed or being treated unfairly. Rather, **I had been given an invitation to "grow."**

Working through my many challenges made me stretch, change, and evolve physically, psychologically, emotionally, and spiritually. As a result, the challenge hasn't gone away. Nothing much about my stature changed at all. What did change was a deepening and strengthening of my capabilities, spiritual connection, and understanding about myself, and my purpose. I deem these gifts invaluable. Now, I feel more fortunate than almost anyone I know.

Today, I appreciate my short stature for it has provided me with an inner depth and richness I might never have known. It has allowed me to see life, myself, and others in a totally different way. Most importantly, it has allowed me to develop and grow in ways I never would have.

From this perspective, I greet the difficulties of my everyday life with more optimism and hope than I did before. I focus on the benefits of my situation more than its detriments. I rejoice in my life and feel blessed to be on earth at this time.

Seeing the gifts within my challenge has been

like having the sun come out after a whole life-time of rain. We might call this an optimistic atti-tude. We might call it positive thinking. We might call it spiritual illumination. Whatever we call it, those who possess a positive attitude toward their challenges have a much greater chance of moving through them with ease and peace.

It was a revelation to realize that pain is not a pun-ishment. No. Pain is a gift. It is a doorway into expan-sion and transformation. It is an invitation to grow and evolve.

If life did not challenge us, we would just sit around eating bon-bons all day. Our difficulties in life call us to go deeper within ourselves. Our challenges force us to develop better skills, more abilities, and new ways of thinking and knowing. They draw forth greater strength and deeper wisdom from our inner selves.

Yes, our challenges are invitations from life. On the surface, they look like doom and horror. However, those who are BIG inside know that underneath a scary façade is a beautiful invitation that says, "Your presence is requested at the party of life! Here is your chance to stretch, grow, and evolve into a BIGGER, better human being!"

If we don't accept the invitation, we don't overcome our pain. If we do accept it and enter into the diffi-culty as it is, we transform from a seed into a most magnificent flower!

So if you have a challenge that feels overwhelming,

know you are an overwhelmingly great human being. No one is given a test without the ability to pass it. Now, you just have to work to change latent abilities into ones you can express.

If you have limitations in your life, know you are not being punished. Rather, you are being encouraged to expand into your HUGE self and WALK TALL. So be BIG! Be courageous! Look that dragon in the eye and you will reap treasures far beyond your wildest imagination!

This list will help you see the gift within your challenges:

1. Trust that the challenge will help you grow and evolve into a BIGGER, better person.
2. Keep your attention on your strengths and your wins.
3. Chart your progress and healing.
4. Appreciate the good things in your life.
5. Take responsibility for yourself and your situation.
6. Surround yourself with positive people.
7. Study, read books and listen to tapes that nurture growth and hope.
8. Maintain optimism when the going really gets tough.

EXERCISE   **Finding the Gift**

In your journal:

1. Draw a vertical line down the middle of a page. At the top of the left-hand column write: "Challenges I faced in the past." On a second

page do the same thing, but title the left-hand column "Challenges I'm dealing with now." Fill in each list.

2. Below each list, write a few words about the *attitude* you have been holding concerning those challenges.

3. In the right-hand column of the first page titled Past Challenges, jot down anything positive that came out of the situation—before, during or after. Did any gifts, seen or unseen, manifest in your life? If so, write them down.

4. Look at your list of current challenges. Are there any gifts you received from your past challenges that might support you in your current ones? If so, write those down in the appropriate places.

5. Now, look at your list of current challenges and speculate what the gift that may come out of this situation could possibly be. Write these in a different color of ink. Look it over and notice how you feel.

6. Write a paragraph or more on how this exercise has affected your current attitude toward your problems. If it helps, read that paragraph once a week, and do this exercise from time to time.

SHIFT YOUR FOCUS

To change your attitude from unhealthy to healthy, from small to BIG, take your focus off the negative stuff, and shift it to the positive. For example, take your attention off the problem and shift it onto the solution. The chart on the following page provides more suggestions.

FOCUS OFF	FOCUS ON
The Differences	The Commonalties
The Disability	The Person
The Problem	The Solution
Fixing Others	Accepting Others As They Are
What Separates Us	What We have In Common
What You Give	What You Get
What Can NOT Change	What You CAN Change
The Weaknesses	The Strengths
The Challenge	The Gift

PERSIST, PERSIST, PERSIST

No one ever climbed to the top of Mount Everest in a day. No one ever learned to play golf in a week. No one ever sailed around the world in a month.

Grand undertakings take time and energy, trial and error, even defeat. The grander the task, the greater the possibility for failure and setback. Thus, the grander the goal, the more we need to persist!

> "
> *What we vividly imagine, ardently desire, and enthusiastically act upon must inevitably come to pass.*
> "
>
> —COLLIN P. SISSON

Keep the goal alive Keeping the goal alive inside of our hearts helps us persist. And when the going gets really tough, we can remind ourselves what we truly want. That will help refuel the engines.

Visualize your goal in your mind. See the place you

want to be. Sit quietly and imagine yourself at the moment of accomplishment. See yourself from different angles and at different times of the day. Imagine how you will feel inside your body at that moment. Summon those feelings as you visualize. Do this frequently. The more you can make the moment of success real inside of you now, the greater your chances of persisting through all the pitfalls and obstacles to get there.

Another way to make the image strong is to make a collage representing your goal. This will help keep it alive in your mind and heart. Create it out of magazine clippings, photographs, or drawings. Put it somewhere you look frequently, like on your refrigerator or mirror. Remember that place—where you want to be—inside of your body, mind *and* soul. All of this will help you get up again when you feel discouraged.

Allow feelings of longing Let yourself experience your desire for your goal. The more deeply you feel your passion, the more steam you will have to climb the mountain. Use your desire as the key to open the door. Never let go of your vision, your dream, or your passion.

I have a friend who has a tendency to give up easily, even with little things. When she meets with a setback, a frustration, or complexity, she throws the bag in and walks away. Her sister behaves much the same. The two of them sit around and make grand plans. Some are creative ventures, some moneymaking schemes, some philanthropic ideas. Plans seem to roll from their lips like water from a fountain.

I hear lots of great plans, but I've never seen one of them accomplished. Why? These sisters have no drive to work hard. They have no gumption to get up after a bad fall. They have no chutzpah to energize the uphill trek. Simply put, they have no persistence-power.

What happens when *you* encounter a bump in the road? Do you collapse and give up? Do you blame someone else and seek revenge? Or do you work hard to find a way to get around, through, under, or over the top of that obstacle? Do you persist?

On the other side of the fence, we have Stu; a hardworking guy whose economic success is the essence of persistence:

Stu arrived in Santa Barbara, California, in 1979, a 24-year-old college graduate. From his early teens, Stu had saved his money earned through newspaper routes, babysitting, and clerking in a store. With those earnings, he bought his first vehicle, a Dodge Van, when he graduated from college. He lived in that van for his first eight months in California, cooking on a Coleman stove every evening under the stars. Stu was happy living simply. He worked at a bicycle shop, and was soon elevated to manager of a branch store. Although his salary topped out at $850 a month, he was able to save $4,000 in those first eight months. He took that money and invested it in his first piece of real estate: a travel trailer.

Living in the trailer for six years, Stu's rent for trailer space had only gone up from a whopping $90 to $150 a month. During that time, he had become a buyer in a natural food store where his salary did not exceed $20,000. Over those six years, Stu lived frugally and saved $30,000. That meant he had enough for the down payment on his first home, a two-bedroom one-bath house in downtown Santa Barbara. In the seven years he lived there, his equity and the local real estate appreciation allowed him to purchase a four-bedroom home in the hills of Santa Barbara where he lives today. That beautiful home has a current estimated value of $1 million.

Stu said, "I knew I wanted financial security in the long run. But mostly, I wasn't sure where I was going or what I needed to do. I did know, however, that if I worked hard and saved my money, when a goal did become clear, the money would be there. And that's what happened. That's how I progressed from one level to the next."

❸

HEALTHY
BELIEFS

BELIEVE IN YOURSELF

Our beliefs are like sunglasses. The color lens we look through paints our world and our experiences. If we look through shades of doom, we get gloom. If we look through shades of sparkling light, we get delight.

> "
> *Whether you believe you can or can't—you're right.*
> "
> —HENRY FORD

Here's the cool thing: we choose. Just like with our thoughts and attitudes. We have the power to choose to believe in ourselves or not. We can put on "I can do it!" glasses, or we can put on "I can't do it" glasses.

Yet, if only it were that simple. Many motivational speakers and authors suggest using affirmations to build yourself up. They suggest saying, writing, reading, and repeating things to yourself like, "I'm great!" "I can do it!" or "I believe in me!" Certainly, this helps. But it doesn't always work. That's because something else is going on beneath the surface that is overpowering our faithful pleas of self-declaration.

A frequent phenomenon that sabotages even the best intentions is holding opposing beliefs about one's self, one in the conscious mind and one in the unconscious mind. For example, you could believe consciously that you are wonderful. But unconsciously, you believe you're inadequate or broken. These varying beliefs about one's self are the very core of the ego structure (our sense of self and identity): deficient underneath, wonderful on the surface.

Conflicting beliefs about our self can be a major obstacle to WALKING TALL, as well as to success and fulfillment in life. Due to their subtle yet powerful nature, beliefs in the unconscious mind ultimately override beliefs in the conscious mind.

So, we must not only encourage ourselves regularly with hearty shouts of "I'm awesome! I believe in ME!" We must also bring our unconscious beliefs about our self into harmony with our enthusiastic affirmations.

Our unconscious beliefs are best expressed through words and actions. So, to discern whether your beliefs are aligned or opposed, observe your behavior and listen to what you say. Do you, at times, express self-doubt? Do you fear being seen by others? Do you sabotage yourself? Do you act self-destructively? Do you say one thing, then do another? If so, you probably hold conflicting beliefs about yourself. Observe your actions and speech. When you catch yourself in a contradiction, take note. Then work to uncover your deeper motivations and beliefs about yourself. Find out where it came from, why it's still there, what is needed. *(For more information on this process, refer to Part III on Inquiry.)*

Believing in ourselves is important because *we* are the main source of support for getting through our difficulties and meeting our goals. And also because we train others how to treat us. People see how we treat ourselves, then follow suit.

Believe in yourself and the world will, too!

ALIGN YOUR BELIEFS AND YOUR DREAMS

Besides believing in ourselves (both consciously and unconsciously), to WALK TALL, we must align what we believe with what we think is possible.

"
Anything is possible.
"
—Deepak Chopra

If you want to be a pilot but don't believe you are smart enough, guess what—it's not likely to happen. If you want to own a home but don't believe you could ever have enough money to buy one, you probably won't.

Again, anyone can rattle off, "I'm smart enough!" or "I CAN earn the money for that house I want," a hundred times a day. That's the easy part. The more challenging part is to expose those beliefs that are working against you and limiting you. You'll find them below the surface of your everyday awareness.

Watch yourself. What beliefs do you hold about

yourself that create a barrier between you and living your dreams? Catch yourself saying or doing something that reveals something contrary to what you think you believe.

Let's say, for instance, your "dream" is to be financially independent so you can sail around the world with your spouse and kids. You are working hard and investing your money to meet your goal. Then one day, you're having lunch with a friend. She says, "What I really want to do is have enough money so I can take my family away from this crazy city life and build a log cabin home in the country. But I've been working for so long and so hard, and I'm still *so far away* from that reality. I just don't think I'll ever pull it off." And you reply, "I know exactly what you mean."

Right there. Right when you said, "I know exactly what you mean," your words expressed doubt. That is your chance to catch yourself and say, "Oh, some part of me evidently doesn't believe I can do it. Where is that coming from?"

Or maybe one Sunday afternoon you find yourself out shopping for your dream house. This behavior goes against your goal of sailing off into the sunset. Take this activity as a big hint. Again, inquire into your motivation and find out more about it. (*Refer to Part III on Inquiry.*)

So watch and listen. Do you truly believe that what you want is possible?

4

HEALTHY
WORDS

SAY WHAT YOU WANT TO CREATE

Speech is a vital link in the process of manifestation, the bridge between what's inside of us and what's outside of us. Speech takes our dream, vision, or goal that is inside and brings it into reality on the outside.

One of the best ways to create the life you want is to use words that describe the life you want. Instead of saying, "I hate my job!" say, "It's time to redesign my job so that it supports me financially *and* makes me happy." Instead of saying, "I never do it right," say, "It didn't work out this time, but next time I'll do better." Instead of saying, "You're impossible!" say, "How can we work this out?"

> "
> Our lives go in the direction of the thoughts inside of our heads and the words that come out of our mouths.
> "
>
> —RICK TAMLIN,
> LIFE-COACH

Listen to yourself as you speak. Do your words reflect what you want? Do they mean what you intend? What impact is your speech having on you, your life, and others?

Speak as though your words are the script of your life. They are! You write the script by the words you choose. So, for a happy, healthy life, choose words that are positive, uplifting, supportive and encouraging.

Nip It in the Bud People who are BIG on the inside understand that positive speech leads to a positive life. Yet, sometimes a negative thought arises, one that is downright cruel and mean. It could be about anything. Maybe it's about you, someone else, or a situation.

We may not have control over that first thought rising up in our awareness. But we do have control over what words come out of our mouths. So, whenever you have a negative thought, it's not a big deal. Just nip it in the bud. Leave it inside and transfix your speech so it generates a positive influence and reflects what you want to bring about.

You could have a negative thought about yourself as you glance into a full-length mirror. The thought bubbles up, "Oh I'm getting so fat!" Because you have been practicing defending against your inner critic, you immediately recognize its presence. You silence it by commanding it to STOP! Then you can look in the mirror again and say what you want to create. Perhaps it's something like: "I'm going to exercise for half an hour every day this month so I can get some of this extra weight off!"

The Impact of Words Have you ever been teased or called nasty names? Has anyone ever yelled at you? Then you know that words spoken can have a huge impact.

When we get upset, angry, or frustrated, it's easy for words that are hurtful to others to slip out. In "hot-head-ed" situations, it's best to be aware of our impact, choose to side step our first impulse, and instead use words that support effective communication.

Let's say you're having an argument with someone. You pay close attention to your words and the tone of voice you use. At a certain point you get really angry. What you *want* to say is: "I hate you when you act like this!" But you catch yourself before the words come out of your mouth. You realize the impact those words will probably have.

So instead you could say: "When you do _____ (name the specific behavior), I get really upset! What would work better is if you would _____ (name the alternative behavior)."

Just because you think it, doesn't mean you have to say it. Part of WALKING TALL is developing the skill of *powerful speech*. That's when our words begin to describe what we want to create in our lives. That's when others understand us when we speak. That's when we articulate with clarity and certainty, and create the impact we intend.

So, choose healthy words and be a positive influence on your life and others' lives, too.

5

HEALTHY
ACTIONS

CREATE SMILING CONSEQUENCES

Every action has an equal and opposite reaction. This is a law of physics. Christ stated the law through the parable, "As you sow, so shall you reap." Eastern religions call it the law of karma—what you do *now* will be done to you *later.*

" As you sow, so shall you reap. "

—THE BIBLE

No matter what you call it, if you believe in it or not, two facts remain:

1. Actions lead to consequences.
2. The nature of a consequence is determined by the nature of the action.

Think of it this way: if you want roses, plant rose seeds.

Even more than our words, our actions have a wide range of influence, many times far beyond what we can perceive. They create an ongoing impact on ourselves, on others, and on our environment, like a pebble dropped into a still lake. The influence of our actions just keeps rippling outwards, and affects ultimately, our whole planet.

What you do to others will eventually be done to you. It doesn't always happen immediately. But sooner or later, you'll find yourself experiencing something very similar to what you did to, or for, someone else.

What you do tells the world who you are. When others observe our behavior, they can assess many things and establish what sort of relationship to have, or not to have, with us.

So take heed. If you want to reap a magnificent harvest, choose magnificent actions. It's that simple—healthy actions beget a healthy life.

TAKE RESPONSIBILITY

Taking responsibility means not blaming others for your lot in life. It means knowing you are responsible for your responses to what happens to you—good or bad. It means acknowledging your power to choose, about your attitudes, beliefs, and actions.

There is a renowned international speaker named W. Mitchell (Mitchell for short). Several years back, Mitchell had a motorcycle accident that left 65% of his body burned. A few years later he became paralyzed from the waist down in a plane crash. (*Down on his luck, I'd say*). But Mitchell never let it get him down. He is a successful businessman, professional speaker, and author. Mitchell's motto through all of it is: "It's not what happens to you, it's what you do about it."

A testimony of the inspiration he gives people all over the world, Mitchell doesn't blame life, God, or others for his fate. He says, "I can focus on the 1000 things I can no longer do. OR I can focus on the 900 things I still can do." Mitchell tells the world he makes a healthy choice by taking responsibility for his attitude and his situation.

As a teenager, I learned how taking responsibility can make you or break you. From childhood, I enjoyed figure skating and was fortunate enough to become quite accomplished at it, winning competitions, and performing in ice shows.

My coach strongly believed in taking responsibility for oneself, only I didn't realize it at the time. He didn't say things like "It's not what happens to you, it's what you do about it." He didn't say, "You are the only one responsible if you fail or succeed." But he did say, "Don't try, just do!" "It's up to you if you land the jump, win the medal,

thrill the crowd, or not!"

I don't think I really appreciated his conviction of "no blame" until the one day I met with a different approach to challenges. That day, engrossed in deep concentration, I was tracing small circles on the ice. A coach whom I respected but didn't know well walked by my "patch" as he sauntered across the rink. He stopped and watched me for a moment. "**If only** you had more length in the middle," he said referring to my torso. "You'd have so much more success tracing your loops perfectly." Then he scuffled off to his next lesson as if nothing had happened.

But something quite serious happened. That phrase never left my mind through the rest of my skating career. Every time I found myself unable to achieve my goal, with a jump or a spin or a figure eight, that phrase would come up in my mind. I did not know how to defend against it. More and more, I blamed my short stature for my lack of successes. I faltered in taking responsibility for myself and my situation. My lack of successes naturally followed suit. Not long after, I quit skating.

Blame comes in many guises. Beware of its devastating effects. Take responsibility. And remember what Mitchell says: "It's not what happens to you, it's what you do about it."

LOVE IT OR CHANGE IT

"If only tomorrow morning I could wake up like Tom Hanks in the movie 'Big', grown to six feet tall overnight! Then all my problems would be over! Then I could be happy!" One day, I found myself admitting this, with great hesitancy, to my Ridhwan teacher Morton, while living in Boulder during my late 30s. He looked at me a long time. I couldn't believe I had said this **out loud.** It seemed I had been holding a version of that confession inside myself for my whole life; I'd only just then became aware of it. I had blurted it out for Morton—and me—to hear.

The silence went on. He finally broke it. "I notice you spend a lot of energy trying to change things that are impossible to change. Don't you get worn down by the futility of it?"

His words hit me like a bucket of ice water, waking me up from a deep trance. I was never able to admit that changing my height was impossible. I couldn't let go of that hope because it always seemed that being average height was the only way to escape all the suffering—the ridicule, the hurt, the shame, the alienation—of being a Little Person.

He continued, "Wouldn't your success rate be much higher if you focused on changing things that you **could** actually change—like your attitudes, your personality, and your beliefs about yourself?"

This rude awakening allowed me to clearly distinguish the difference—the difference between what I had to accept and what I had to **change**. Right then, I decided to stop fantasizing about changing my height and to shift my focus onto changing things about myself that I could change.

That commitment took me through a lot of changes. I worked hard to transform my self-worth, my attitude, and my ability to accept myself. I stopped whining and complaining. I increased my ability to stay focused and function in the world. And, eventually, I gained the skills and confidence to begin helping others. These are things I **could** change.

Nowadays, I can't imagine believing that being average height was the only thing that would grant me happiness. I realize, with humility, that if I had become average size without changing anything about **me**, I'd still be miserable. I'd still be full of inner smallness. It was changing the things I

*could change that allowed my nightmare to turn
into a celebration. Thank you, God, for giving me
the wisdom to know the difference.*

Change What You Can Change

We have many options for change—no matter what
our situation. We all have the ability to become empowered, courageous, successful, and happy. In other
words, we all have the power to WALK TALL.

It's true that we cannot change who our family
members are, but we *can* change who our friends and
associates are. We may not be able to change that we
have an illness, but we *can* change our daily health
practices. In most cases, we can't change our disability, but we can increase our skills, talents, and education. We can turn our focus off what we *cannot* do and
on to what we *can* do; off what we *don't* have and on
to what we *do* have. Many times we can't change the
pain our loved ones endure, but we can sit and be with
them, extend our compassion, nourish them, and
remind them they are loved. We can't control how people respond to us, but we can control how tall we
stand, how much self-pride we embody, and how we
respond to another's small-mindedness.

Some people say that innate intelligence cannot be
altered. True or not, you can always learn more, work
and study harder, apply yourself more diligently. You
can persist. If you experience oppression and prejudice,
go where less exists. Change your locality; alter the
neighborhood you live in. If you don't like the way you

look—change it! Lose some weight. Get a new hairstyle. Buy some new clothes that flatter you. Learn how to apply makeup so it enhances your good looks.

Sometimes it's difficult to change. But as Eleanor Roosevelt says: "You must do the things you think you can not do."

Here's a chart that outlines certain things we can and cannot change:

CANNOT CHANGE	CAN CHANGE
Family: Parents, Kids, Relatives	Friends, Associates
Outer Size	Inner Size
Illness	Habits For Healthy Living
Disability	Skills, Talents, Education, Focus
Race	Resume, Attitude, Personality
Cultural Background	Lifestyle
Others' Pain	Others' Sense of Isolation
Others' Responses To Us	How We Respond
Challenges Given to Us	Attitude About Our Challenges
Innate Intelligence/ Creativity	How Hard We Study/ Practice/Work
Past Situations	Present and Future Situations
Oppression from Others	Where We Live and Hang Out, Personal Empowerment
Basic Physique	Weight, Clothing, Hair, Style, Make-Up

EXERCISE   What I Can Change

1. Ask yourself, "What would I like to change about myself or my life that would make me happier?" Answer the question writing in a stream of con-

sciousness. Include all the things you don't like about yourself, your relationships, your work or home environment, and anything else you can think of.

2. Now, on a separate page, draw a vertical line down the middle. Referring to the things you have just written, list the ones you *cannot* change in the left-hand column. In the right column, list those you *can* change.

3. From your list of things that you *can* change, choose three things you *want* to change in the near future, things you'd like to work on now. Underline or circle those three things.

4. Make a plan and begin changing what you *can change* in your self and your life. *(Part I, Chapter 8 called Creating The Life You Want, will give you more information about this process.)*

5. When you feel ready to change a few more things about yourself or your life, go back to your list and pick three more things to work on, or repeat this exercise.

ACCEPT WHAT YOU CAN'T CHANGE

I love Oprah. I love her vision, her willingness to work hard, and her dedication to improving the quality of people's lives.

Oprah made a movie recently about her struggle with her weight and how she overcame it. Both inspirational and instructional, it has probably helped thousands of women lose weight.

As I watched the show, however, I kept thinking,

"What about people like me? What about people who are different because of something that they **cannot** change? What about the woman who is missing her right leg, or the young girl whose face got badly burnt, or all the people in wheelchairs? Is there any hope for us? Can we ever be happy?"

I knew the answer, of course, was yes. Everyone can be happy because happiness is an inner condition, not an outer. Happiness is present when we feel BIG inside, and is held at bay when we feel small.

How do we accept something we don't want to accept? How do we let go of hope when hope appears to be the only solution? These are not easy questions to answer.

First, as we become empowered, we improve our lives—we take on a healthy attitude, defend against the inner critical voice, change those things that we can change. All of these fertilize positive experiences and feelings. As life becomes rosier, it becomes easier to accept the things we cannot change.

Second, working with emotions can help. In my inner growth process, I allowed a lot of my sadness and hurt to come up to the surface. It melted the ice around my heart and compassion began to flow, not only for my own limitations and hardships, but for those of others as well.

One day toward the beginning of my work with my Ridhwan teacher Morton, I was upset because my love life was so incredibly painful. I had experienced so many failures, felt so many rejections. That day, Morton asked me to really feel my sadness. I said, "I have been. I've been sitting here telling you all about it." He replied, "You have been talking about it, not **feeling** it. Now, stop talking and just feel what's in your heart."

I closed my eyes and focused on my heart. With my inner vision I saw my heart as a battlefield. For miles, swords and knifes of all kinds were stabbing into the ground, my heart. I said, "My heart is a battlefield of wounds." Then I began to feel it—the deep, excruciating pain that had been held inside for so long. My tears flowed in streams.

After several minutes of letting the sadness move through me (and blowing my nose), Morton asked me to look into my heart again. This time I saw an emerald green mist floating all around my heart. The feeling that emanated from it was soft and gentle. It passed over my entire body, soothing the upset. I felt washed clean of all the pain by a strong and undeniable sense of compassion. I felt held by this gentle presence, like a mother's embrace, and felt empathy for what I had had to endure. It rippled out, expanding until I felt compassion for the hardships all people endure. I no longer felt alone and isolated. I felt connected to everyone, because everyone bears pain of some sort.

With this sense of peace, I was much better able to begin letting go of my resentment about my situation and accept myself as I am. I left Morton's office that day feeling incredibly tender, an unusual sensation for me. I smiled as I placed my hand softly over my heart. I appreciated the gift that had arisen out of my challenge.

Third, accepting what we can't change many times calls for a spiritual treatment. Challenges such as the one I described here are given to us so we can go deeper inside of ourselves. They make us stretch, grow, and increase our sense of inner depth and enlightenment. They help us connect to a more essential, spiritual part of ourselves, as this experience did for me. Sometimes the things that we can't change require prayer, a prayer for grace or guidance. And sometimes they require surrender.

It's never easy, but learning to accept the difficult things as they are is perhaps the biggest personal and spiritual triumph we can have. It is also the sure mark of a BIG person.

Here's an exercise to clarify where you are in this process.

EXERCISE Nurturing Acceptance

1. Go back to the list you made earlier on things

you cannot change. Scrutinize each item, carefully determining whether it is impossible to change, or whether it might just be very difficult to change. If you find anything in your left-hand list that you can move over to your "things I can change" list, cross it out and add it to your "can change" list. If you're list is on the computer, just cut and paste.

2. Now look at your list of things you cannot change. Just sit with it for a while. Notice what thoughts and feelings well up inside. Record your feelings on a separate piece of paper.

3. Write down the following questions and their answers. Be as honest as you can.

a. How do I feel about the things in my life that I cannot change?

b. Am I in denial about them? Or have I been aware of them for some time?

c. What level of acceptance do I have for them? Give them a rating, 1 being low and 10 being high.

d. What more can I do to grow acceptance for these things?

e. Am I at peace about these things?

4. When you have answered these questions, access where you are in the process of growing acceptance for the things in your life you cannot change.

5. Think of one or two things you would like to do to nurture your capacity to accept these things. Write them here. Check back in a few weeks and report in your journal how you are coming along in the process. Are you "growing" acceptance? Or do you need to try a different tactic? If so, what will you do now?

❻

HEALTHY
BODY

MEET YOUR BODY'S NEEDS

Our bodies transport us through life. They take us from place to place and ground our experiences. Our physical state of health intimately links to our well-being. Therefore, a healthy body generates a sharp mind, a positive attitude, and a happy mood.

The opposite is also true.

Meeting our bodies' needs can be a demanding and time-consuming job. Every day, they need a variety of fresh and cooked foods plus exercise, sleep, water, and sunlight. They need to be washed and kept warm or cool, as the case might be. They also need a lot of love from us to meet all those nagging requirements. Just like caring for children, the more our bodies receive what they need when they need it, the more cooperative and healthy they become in the long run.

Every human body has limitations that must be respected. Some of us need more rest than others; some more exercise or more fluids. We differ in our physical dispositions and our unique health requirements. We can read books about general rules for good health, but ultimately, we each have differing needs. The solution is to tune into our bodies and pay attention to what they tell us.

Sometimes they say, "Enough exercise for today," "Stop eating. I'm full now," or "I need some protein!" The more we respond to these subtle—and not so subtle—requests our bodies send, the healthier and more vital they will become.

Even though our bodies constantly talk to us about what they need, we don't always respond accordingly. For example, when you get a cold, your body may be saying, "I need more rest." But if you don't give yourself more rest, a few weeks later, your body speaks up again, this time a bit louder. "I need more rest!" Now you have bronchitis. You take medication to cover the symptoms, continue staying out late, getting up early, and working or playing too hard. The following week, your body shouts at you. "I NEED MORE REST!!" Now you have pneumonia. If you don't respond this time and give your body more rest, you will end up with an illness that totally immobilizes you.

The more sensitively and timely you respond to your body's needs, the healthier it becomes. Respect your body's limitations and it will give you all it has to give. Respond to its needs and watch your spirit soar!

EAT, DRINK (WATER), SLEEP, AND BE MERRY

EAT The food we eat nourishes us and gives us energy to do what we want to do. It influences our whole self because the state of our physical body affects our mental, emotional, and spiritual bodies as well.

So let's take a look at what kind of eating habits support a healthy body.

• **Eat fresh and whole foods, organic if possible.** These types of foods provide our bodies with the maximum amount of nutrients and vitamins. Heavily processed foods such as prepared and packaged food have been stripped of their nutritious value. Choose whole grains over refined flour, fresh fruits and vegetables over those that have been canned, packaged or frozen. Bake, grill, poach, or broil your foods. Throw away the "frying" pan.

• **Prepare delicious, well-balanced meals at home.** Get a cookbook filled with recipes of the type of food you love. Try some of the recipes preparing your favorite veggies or meats in a variety of ways. Your meals should contain some protein (meat, eggs, fish, or tofu), some carbohydrate (veggies, starches and fruits), and a little fat (butter or oil). When you take time to prepare good food, it is an incredible act of self–love that nourishes both body and soul.

• **Eat when you are hungry.** Everyone has different needs around when to eat and how much food is required. Tune in to your body, not the clock, to determine when you need to eat. Also listen to what kinds of foods your body wants and refrain from grabbing tempting items in front of you.

• **Stop eating when you are full.** Imagine your stomach is a container that has ten levels: "one" being starving hungry and "ten" being after-Thanksgiving-dinner-full. The time to eat is when you get down to "two" or less. The time to stop eating is when you get filled up to "five," that is half full. This helps you maintain or regain your "natural" body form.

• **Listen to your body.** There are as many theories on what foods create optimal health as there are stars in the sky. How do you know which one is best for you? By trying the most appealing ones and paying attention to how you feel. Does this group of foods make you feel energized or sluggish, happy or sad, light or heavy? Do you easily digest these foods? Do you like the taste? How does it affect your work and sleep? Find the way of eating that suits you best. You can only assess this by listening to what your body tells you.

EXERCISE The human body is meant to move. Only in the last 100 years or so have people used mechanical forms of transportation. For all of history, humans have moved on land primarily through the power of their own legs. Our bodies are designed to move on a regular basis. That's why we exercise.

"Eat less; exercise more." This is the formula for losing excess weight. The recipe is simple. The hard part is staying with it. Regular exercise is necessary in keeping our hearts strong and muscles mighty. In our modern-day lifestyle of sitting, sitting, and more sitting, it's important to make a concerted effort to be physically active for 30 minutes or more at least three times a week.

Suggestions for getting more exercise:

1. Find a sport or physical workout program that is really fun.

2. Get a friend to join you in doing it.

3. Mark your calendar with your physical activity or workout time.

4. Commit to showing up for your exercise appointment.

5. Eat fresh and light foods. Heavily processed and fatty foods make you feel sluggish and sleepy. Fresh foods energize you; then you feel like being active.

SLEEP Sleep when you are tired. Sleep is often overlooked as an ingredient to having a healthy body. You know you're getting an adequate amount of sleep when you experience clarity of mind, equanimity of emotions, and a deep sense of spiritual connection. When you are tired, nothing feels enjoyable. You can't work or play well; you experience low energy and a foggy mind. Your level of alertness affects how you see the world, how you feel about things, people, and yourself. Conversely, being well rested leads to happiness and well-being.

Most experts say adults need eight hours of sleep a night. If you skip or miss some sleep, you will have sleep debt. Accumulated sleep debt can lead to numerous physical, psychological, and emotional problems.

Suggestions for getting more sleep:

1. Nap. Naps are a great way make up some sleep debt. Whatever time of the day, if you feel tired, take a few minutes and lie down. Sleep for a few minutes or a half an hour. See how refreshed and awake you feel afterwards.

2. Go to bed earlier or wake up later.

3. Rearrange your daily and evening activities to allow more time for sleep.

4. Turn off the TV earlier than usual and just read. See if less stimulation in the night results in your feeling a need to sleep more readily.

5. Get enough physical activity in the day so your body is tired when you get into bed.

6. Eat lighter in the evening and avoid foods that upset your stomach.

7. Take public transportation or a car pool to and from work so you can nap while in transit.

DRINK WATER   Drink eight glasses of fresh spring water a day.

The body is about 70 percent water. Its water supply is responsible for every function including digestion, absorption, circulation, and excretion. It transports nutrients, maintains your body's temperature and carries out waste. Therefore, the water used in sweat and elimination needs to be replaced often.

Water that runs through the tap can contain run-off from farm chemicals and environmental pollutants. Drinking filtered or bottled water is far safer and healthier. Coke, diet Sprite, coffee, and the like do not count as healthy drinks because they alter the body's chemistry like drugs do. They do not contribute to a healthy body in any way so they cannot be considered part of a healthy diet.

Suggestions for increasing your daily water intake:

1. Keep a jug of spring water handy in your refrigerator so when you need something cool to drink, you can reach in and it's ready to go.

2. At a restaurant, order sparkling water instead of coke; order herbal tea instead of coffee or black tea.

3. Carry a bottle of water with you when you leave the house. Keep a jug in your car and refill as needed.

4. When you go to a meeting, fill your glass with water and be sure to drink it before you leave the room.

5. Get up and refill your glass when it is empty.

6. Drink a bottle of water when you play sports or work out.

7. Fill up a large glass of water and set it in front of you wherever you watch TV. Finish your water before you turn the TV off.

SUNLIGHT People need sunshine. Sunlight affects your emotions and spirits, too. Getting out in the sunshine can be challenging since many folks work indoors, do their exercise programs indoors, watch TV or movies indoors, sit at their computers, cook their meals...all indoors. Even driving in a car doesn't provide much sunshine.

Suggestions for getting more sunlight:

1. Do your exercise program outdoors at least one day a week. Ride your bike, jog, or walk outside during the day instead of in the gym.

2. Park your car in the farthest space from your work place entrance or a block or more from your home.

3. Take your (or your neighbor's) dog for a walk.

4. Spend time working in your garden.

5. Sit outside to read, chat, or dine.

6. Meet a friend for a walk in the park or on a hiking trail instead of at a restaurant.

7. Choose restaurants with outdoor seating and sit outside.

STIMULANTS: nicotine, caffeine & sugar People like stimulants because they give them a "buzz." Yet stimulants alter your body's chemistry just like drugs do and change the way you feel. Most people get a positive or "high" feeling from these substances. Though they make you feel good, beware. They can be addictive and do not support having a healthy body.

• **Nicotine** Nicotine is definitely addictive. Smoking cigarettes kills. Listed in my thesaurus under "tobacco," are the synonyms: filthy weed, coffin nails, and cancer sticks. Why even consider smoking? Because it's cool? Because you're already hooked and can't stop? Whatever your reason, does it justify throwing away your good health and quickening your death sentence? I doubt it.

Suggestions to decrease/quit your nicotine intake:

1. Just say no! Create healthy boundaries.

2. When you get the urge for a smoke, first take five deep slow breaths of fresh air, then see if the urge is still there. (Most people who are addicted crave the calming effect that comes with the deep inhalations. So breathe fresh air instead of smoke and get what you want that way.)

3. Join and regularly attend a support group for quitting smoking.

4. Practice yoga and deep breathing on a regular basis.

5. Smoke one less cigarette a day until you're down to "none" a day.

6. Stop hanging around people who think it's cool to poison their bodies by breathing in a "parasite" that feeds on their lungs.

7. Create a ritual in which you throw away all your cigarettes and commit to quitting. Having a friend join you in this can be supportive and more fun.

• **Caffeine** Caffeine is a strong stimulant that over activates the adrenal glands. This revving up of the system puts us into a "fight or flight" response. (Why anybody wants to generate the feeling they need to fight or run for their life is beyond me.)

Caffeine is present in all coffee, less powerful in decaf. It is also present in all black and green teas. Drinking these fluids on a daily basis can overwork the adrenals as well as the heart. This can result in a loss of vitality, efficiency, and health in both these chief body parts.

Coffee culture is extremely prevalent in Western

Europe and has gained popularity in remarkable strides in the U.S. Coffeehouses are the urban replacement for a walk in the woods—a time to chill out and take it easy, a place to meet friends, to write, and to read. The social allure of the coffeehouse may be more attractive than the coffee itself. But once they've got you there, most people have to have their java!

Suggestions to decrease caffeine consumption:
1. Have herbal tea instead of coffee or black tea.
2. Have a latté instead of an espresso.
3. Have decaf, instead of the leaded version.
4. Cut down your intake by at least one cup a week.
5. Try different teas or coffee substitutes (like Tachino, Rostaroma, or Postum) until you find one you like as much (okay, almost as much) as your java, then drink that as an alternative.
6. Meet a friend or read your book in the park instead of at a coffeehouse.
7. As you walk by a coffee establishment, enjoy the aroma of the coffee and let that be enough.

• **Sugar** Sugar has a similar revving up effect on the body as does caffeine. It overworks the adrenal glands which throws many vital functions out of whack. It may not give as noticeable of a "buzz" as caffeine does. However, sugar is everywhere. It's rare to find packaged food that does not have sugar in it. In a mini-mart shop, it may be impossible to locate a single food substance that does not have sugar as the number one ingredient.

Sugar is in all prepared desserts and pastries. Sugar is in gum, candy, and breakfast cereals. It is in most all prepared and packaged foods. All soft drinks are loaded with sugar, or worse yet, sugar substitutes. Sugar substitutes are fake food. They have no nutritional value and, in many cases, can cause very harmful diseases like cancer. Fruits and fruit juices contain natural sugar and are a good substitute for sugary desserts and sodas.

Soda pops such as Coke, Sprite and root beer contain more than 40 grams, or eleven teaspoons, of sugar EACH. This is an incredible amount of sugar! How many teaspoons of sugar are required in our daily nutritional allowance? None. White sugar is a *highly* refined derivative of sugar cane. All its nutritional qualities have been stripped away. What ends up in the common sugar bowl is not a food. It's a drug.

Parents often don't realize that high amounts of sugar in children over-stimulate their adrenal glands making them abnormally active, wired, moody, and uncooperative. The same is true for adults, but the behaviors are usually more pronounced in children. Parents give their children soda pop or large desserts in the evening and wonder why they don't want to go to bed or can't fall asleep. Children who take in too much sugar on a daily basis can develop emotional and/or psychological problems as well as premature obesity and type-two diabetes. Parents: carefully monitor your child's intake of sugar keeping it at a minimum!

When digested, carbohydrates (pasta, potatoes, and breads) turn into sugar. So, although a plate of pasta may not taste as sweet as a ripe peach or a piece of cake, once it gets inside your stomach, your body doesn't know the difference. So curb those carbs!

Overuse of sugar or carbohydrates can give rise to: type II diabetes, obesity, tooth and gum decay, coronary problems, varicose veins, and more. Type II diabetes can lead to other serious health issues such as blindness, kidney disease, and loss of nerve functioning. Sugar is also addictive, so it's very important to enjoy it in moderation.

Suggestions for decreasing sugar in your diet.

1. Drink water or juice, preferably fresh vegetable or fruit juice, instead of soda pop.

2. Don't buy any food from a mini-mart.

3. When you are baking, put in half the amount of sugar the recipe suggests.

4. Cut in half the amount of sugar you use in your coffee.

5. Eat a piece of fruit instead of dessert.

6. Eat half a portion of dessert instead of the whole thing, and eat it more slowly, enjoying the taste more attentively.

7. Decrease your portions of breads, pasta, and potatoes by half, or more.

8. At meals, eat greater amounts of non-starchy vegetables and protein foods than carbohydrates.

9. Eat sugar (foods or drinks) only after you have had a meal of "real food," of protein and vegetables.

10. Use honey or real maple syrup (whole foods) to sweeten your foods in place of white sugar.

7

HEALTHY
RELATIONSHIPS

HANG OUT WITH PEOPLE WHO SUPPORT YOU

If you want your plants to grow, you place them in the sun and give them water, right? Similarly, if you want to grow—to get BIG on the inside and WALK TALL—then you place yourself in an environment that gives you the nourishment you need. Hang out with folks who say

"
I get by with a little help from my friends.
"
—LENNON/MCCARTNEY

nice things, give you compliments, commend your work, reward your efforts, and praise you for being who you are.

Healthy relationships are key to learning how to WALK TALL. It's not easy to do any of the things we've been talking about. And it's all the more difficult when we are doing them alone.

Everybody needs a cheering section. No matter if

you're down-and-out or swinging from the top, people feel better, stronger, and more optimistic when they know they are loved and valued.

How many people are in the world? Billions! You can choose to be around whomever you like. So, if you find yourself trapped in a relationship(s) where you are withering in the dark, remember the six billion other choices you have available to you.

Minimize your time with folks who bring you down, criticize or abuse you, or don't treat you well. Choose instead to hang out with people who are like sunshine, who shower you freely with admiration, love, and support.

We all need people to let us know we are fabulous, wonderful, and magnificent, because we are! So, make the choice to be with people who make you feel loved!

I learned that from one of my first sunny friends:

It was a snowy, typically gray Midwest Sunday afternoon. My folks had bundled three-year-old me in a puffy pink thermal suit. I felt more like a mummy than a kid, as I could barely bend my arms or legs. We drove over to our friend's house, but instead of going inside, we sat outside on an old rickety bench. My mom strapped these pink plastic things to the soles of my boots. I looked down and saw two silver blades, side by side, beneath each foot.

What? I wondered. Before I knew it, my dad had picked me up and placed me on the frozen pond in front of us. Then he took my hand and shouted,

"Let's skate!"

I looked around and saw all the big kids zooming by like soaring birds. I'm not sure if I was frozen from bewilderment or fear. My dad tossed me a reassuring wink and gently squeezed my hand. Then he picked up one knee at a time, showing me how I could skate. I began to pick up my knees, too, and together we marched like soldiers across the ice.

After a while, my mother joined us, taking my other hand. Then I could really skate! The three of us toddled around and around that frozen pond, my smile growing wider with each circle we made. By the end of the afternoon, I could march across the ice all by myself. That day, I discovered my first love: ice-skating.

After several requests, my mom finally signed me up for skating lessons when I was six. The rink was about the size of our garage. My best friend Mary Sullivan and her sister Julie joined me in this grand adventure. Before class, we'd wrestle with our long white laces. Then, with all our concentration, we'd attempt to make it across the rink without falling down!

Mary, Julie, and I soon graduated to an Olympic-sized rink. Every Saturday morning, we'd scuffle round and round, gliding on one foot, attempting to stop, and giggling madly as we wiggled our bottoms to propel ourselves backwards. Over the next few years, the three of us earned badges in every color of the rainbow.

In fourth grade, I began private lessons and, that year, transformed into a real skater—doing spins and jumps. In May, our club put on an ice show to raise funds for Olympic skaters. Its theme was the circus and I was the elephant trainer. I remember laughing through all my rehearsals because my instructor, Pieter Kollen, totally cracked me up. He choreographed a great routine for me, ending it with a "shoot-the-duck" between the legs of the ele-phant—cheerfully exploiting my uniqueness!

PEGGY O'NEILL
ELEPHANT TRAINER

Returning in the fall, I began taking lessons from Mr. Kollen. Pieter had been a national skating champion, and working with him demanded a whole new level of commitment. Although he had a fabulous sense of humor and always made me laugh, Pieter demanded hard work and dedication to the sport.

Thursday became my favorite day of the week because that was the day of my lessons. I always looked forward to spending time with him.

Together, we'd polished my spins and perfected my form. Sometimes he was serious and would focus on mastering skills. Sometimes we would giggle as he teased me about my many "fanny busters." I just loved to be with him. He was a best friend (only he was an adult).

Mr. Kollen wore the costume of a skating coach—long heavy coat, rubber-soled boots, and a steaming cup of coffee in hand. He stood by the boards and gave lessons. He looked like a coach, but his ability to see the good in people made him infinitely more than a coach.

In the ten years we worked together, Mr. Kollen never seemed to doubt for a moment my ability to become a champion skater. He never saw my stature as an obstacle to my success, only my wavering willingness to work hard.

His belief in me quietly strengthened my confidence and courage. It allowed me to compete, to perform in ice shows, and to get out there every day and do my best. Mr. Kollen taught me to fight for what I wanted and think like a champion. While struggling to land a new jump, he'd say, "There is no trying. There is just DOING!"

My success as a figure skater provided a splendid antidote to the difficult experiences I endured growing up. My skating trophies triumphed over all that *ugliness. And Mr. Kollen gave me the greatest gift of all: belief in myself, no matter what the obstacles, no excuses. "I am a human being with enormous capacity! Whatever I want to do, I can do!"*

When you find people who believe in you, stick with them, respect them, and most of all, never forget them.

SET BOUNDARIES

Part of WALKING TALL is learning how to set boundaries—letting other people know how much physical space you need around you to feel comfortable and safe.

For example, you're out on a date and the person you are with wants to get closer than feels comfortable to you. Being able to say "stop" or "stay away" is important in these situations and strongly supports building appropriate relationships.

Stand with both arms, shoulder height, reaching from your sides. Stretch your fingers. Now turn in place until your fingertips have traced a circle around your body space, or boundary. Then with your hands, paint in an imaginary wall from head to toe. That is your body's "boundary."

We all have a circumference of space that surrounds us; it provides protection from the outer world. In any given situation, the amount of space we need to feel safe can expand or contract. Usually, the closer we are with someone emotionally, the smaller the amount of space between one another is desired. With strangers and people we don't care for, we prefer a larger, thicker boundary.

Sometimes people come inside our boundaries against our will. This is a violation, so you need to let them know they have to step back. You have the right to set a boundary any time and with whomever you want. You are the boss of you. So, take responsibility for asking others to give you more space when you need it. That's WALKING TALL.

Saying "no" to doing things you don't want do is another form of setting boundaries and WALKING TALL. It is an important part of self-empowerment and an act of self-love, as it means that honoring yourself has become more important than pleasing others. You nurture yourself by doing *only* the things you *want* to do. And you honor others by letting them know what they can expect from you.

We also have emotional boundaries we need to assert and protect. Many times people will make statements that hurt us. They may be direct or indirect. They could be about us, about someone else, or even about a situation. They could be frank or sarcastic, serious or joking. Whatever the case, another's comments can upset us and hurt our feelings.

You can set healthy, fair boundaries by letting others know that what they said offended you. Frequent replies after hearing such feedback are: "Oh, you're just too sensitive. Lighten up. It was a joke." But to you it was not funny; it was hurtful.

Here's the deal. Sensitivity is a grand thing. It allows

you to FEEL life. Without the ability to feel, people are just machines—empty, hollow boxes that walk around. You have a right to feel your life experiences, yourself, and the impact of those around you. You have the right to let others know they are being offensive. You have the right to assert your emotional boundaries by honoring your sensitivity and asking others to be more gentle, cautious, respectful, and/or caring.

Be courageous and strong! Make space for yourself by saying the big "N.O." to what you don't want to do. Let others know when their words or mannerisms are hurtful. Setting boundaries is a great way to practice personal empowerment and to WALK TALL!

INVEST IN APPROPRIATE RELATIONSHIPS

Believe it or not, it is possible to love everyone and everything unconditionally. It only requires establishing the correct distance, or the appropriate relationship, to everyone and everything.

Here on planet Earth, we have all kinds of people. For the sake of simplicity, let's say people are good, bad, or a mixture of the two. Each person has his/her own combination of each—some are 40% good and 60% bad, some 90/10, some 70/30. Let's call these their ratings. Relationships feel best when we are close to those who have a similar rating as we have, and we are farther away from those whose ratings are vastly different from ours. In such cases, it's antagonistic, like oil and water.

Healthy relationships, therefore, are *appropriate* relationships that align with who you are. So the clue is to objectively assess your level of alignment with another person, then establish the closeness of the relationship based on that assessment.

I'm sure that sounds confusing, but it's not really difficult to do. Simply pay attention to what your feelings tell you and you'll sense the accurate level of alignment.

Let's look at a step-by-step process:

1. **Ask yourself, "How does this person make me feel?"**
2. **Be impeccably honest in your response.**
3. **When it is positive, nurture the relationship.**
4. **When it doesn't feel good, ask the person to change their behavior, or create some distance.**
5. **If the person doesn't change, create distance.**

1. Ask yourself, "How does this person make me feel?" When you are with someone, ask yourself this question. Pay attention to what s/he does and how you are treated. Notice how this person affects you. Repeat the question to yourself in a myriad of situations: while you're alone, at a family gathering, hanging out with kids, or dealing with daily tasks. Just keep noticing if it feels good or bad to be with any particular person. This technique can be used on all types of relationships: new ones, old ones, current ones, romantic relationships, business associates, or friendships.

Let's ascertain the answer from three centers in the body:

1. Mind (that discriminates hot from cold, white from black)
2. Heart (that connects and unifies)
3. Belly (that feels what is going on)

Your belly center is the most important in this particular task. It is the center that accesses how you really feel about people and things. It also connects you to your inner guidance and intuition. *(If you'd like information on how to open and/or strengthen your belly center, please refer to Part III, the Kath Meditation.)*

2. Be impeccably honest in your response. This process works only in proportion to how honestly you answer the question: how does this person make me feel? You are the only one who needs to know the answer; nobody's feelings will get hurt. Just notice to *yourself* the answer to this question.

It's often difficult to be honest about our true response to others. Why? Because the greater our need for love, the harder it is to be honest—objective—when answering the question.

People who have been single or in a bad relationship for a prolonged period, or kids who have uncaring parents, have a huge need for love and intimacy. We all have this need, but their's has been exasperated over time. Feeling a great hunger, they tend to gobble up the first sign of love that comes along.

So often I hear stories about people who hop in the sack with someone they have only gone out with once or twice. Then two months later, they are broken hearted because this person, whom they thought was so wonderful, turns out to be a real jerk.

They simply didn't take the time to determine their degree of alignment with this person. Instead, they established an immediate closeness, certainly physically and probably emotionally, with little or no information about how it *really* feels to be with this person over time.

An appropriate relationship has everything to do with the proper amount of distance or closeness you have with others based on the degree of alignment. **When the distance is correct, the love can flow effortlessly.**

If you feel especially hungry for love, which most people do, exercise caution and "look before you leap." Acknowledge your hunger, yet do your best to extend your fast a little longer. Get the information you need to discern. In the long run, it will save many heartaches and unnecessary difficulties for both you and those close to you.

Make the truth your friend. Tell the truth the best you can, because it is the light that will guide you into healthy and happy relationships.

3. When it feels good, nurture the relationship. So, you're hanging out with someone you just met. You ask yourself, "How does this person make me feel?" and the answer is "good." You take a step closer. You spend more time together. Then the answer becomes, "It feels really good to be with this person. He treats me well and lets me know he cares about me." You let him come a step closer to you. You spend more time, and then more yet. Now you ascertain: "I can *trust* this person. That feels great!" You move closer still.

When the answer to "the question" is predominantly positive, nurture the relationship: open up step by step, spend more time together, share from a deeper place, show you care. However, when the answer is, "No, this person doesn't feel so good to be around," take a step back: spend less time together, share from a more superficial place, keep a distance.

This is the basic dance of relationships: drawing closer together or farther apart. You make these movements based on how much you enjoy being with one another. You've been doing this dance your whole life. Only now, you're doing it with more awareness, honesty, and intention.

Sometimes folks ask me, "How long does it take to know if you're aligned with someone or not? When will I know our appropriate relationship?" Every situation is different. I can't say when you will know. But I can say you can't possibly know in less than a few months. True character, level of integrity, and another's dark side takes months to be revealed. And these are things you need to know about someone before determining how closely you are aligned and how close you want to get.

Here are two lists of questions to help determine how it feels to be with someone and how aligned you are. The information in one list will give you information for the other. Feel free to add your own questions to the lists. Remember to keep your belly center open so you can feel what is really going on.

EXERCISE   Aligned or Not?

FEELING:

- How much fun do I have with this person?
- How much do we laugh when we're together?
- Does s/he treat me the way I like to be treated?
- Is it easy to get along with this person?
- Do we share a mutual interest, or is it one-sided? How does that feel?
- Is s/he negative or controlling?
- What kind of mood is s/he in most of the time?
- Can s/he have a serious conversation some of the time?
- Can s/he lighten up and have fun?
- Does s/he withhold affection or give it abundantly?
- Is s/he distracted easily?
- Does s/he flirt?
- Are my needs being met?

_____

_____

_____

_____

ALIGNMENT:

- How caring is this person?
- Does s/he seem interested in me, my life, my goals, my dreams?
- What interests do we share?
- Are our long-term goals aligned?
- Is her/his life headed in a similar direction as mine?
- How well does s/he communicate?

- How dependable is s/he?
- How well does s/he take care of her/himself?
- Is where s/he wants to be in 10 (25, 40) years where I want to be in 10 (25, 40) years? (This question is more for people interested in marriage.)
- How successfully does s/he deal with her/his responsibilities?
- How does this person handle money and financial debt?
- What are the strong and weak points of this person's personality?
- Does s/he work hard?
- How does s/he deal with conflict?
- How does this person deal with anger, challenges, and frustrations?
- What's her/his relationship with drugs, alcohol, food, sex, and work?
- Is this person an addict?
- How does that work for me? (It's wise to ask this question after any of the questions listed.)

_____

_____

_____

_____

_____

_____

_____

_____

You can notice all these characteristics from the onset of any relationship. Pay attention and let your feelings guide you.

4. When it doesn't feel good, ask the person to change their behavior, or create some disstance. Many times in the course of a growing relationship, we discover certain behaviors in the other person that are difficult to tolerate. Perhaps she is flirtatious or works too much. Maybe he's uncaring or lies frequently. You may adore each other and have a fabulous time together. An investment has been made, it is paying off, but there is a thorn. In such cases, you have a choice: to create distance in the relationship, or to ask for a change in behavior.

Some people think to ask loved ones, good friends, or business associates to change is unthinkable. This is only true in *dysfunctional* relationships. In healthy relationships, you can dialogue about how the relationship is going, how it feels, if it's working, and if any adjustments need to be made.

> During my years as a psychotherapist, a divorced client once told me that every New Year's Eve she and her husband would each share ONE thing they wanted the other to change. This was their big "bringing in the new" ritual. That's when they let it all hang out. The rest of the year, neither uttered a word along these lines.
>
> I was shocked! I thought, I'm lucky if I can make it through a week without talking to my husband about making some adjustments in his behavior, and the same for him. I wondered how could they hold

their discomfort inside for so long? Who were they
trying to impress by being so polite? Looking back, it's
not a big mystery that they didn't make it as a couple.

Keeping the lines of communication open more than one evening a year, is a HUGE asset to any relationship. Often, however, people avoid these conversations because they can hurt the others feelings and/or bring up hostile defenses. *So*, to keep those hurts and defenses to a minimum, try a gentle approach.

Here are some guidelines that might help:

SUPPORTIVE	UNSUPPORTIVE
Start the conversation when everyone is calm and you have some privacy.	Starting the conversation when either is angry, frustrated, or around other people.
Speak with a soft, gentle voice. Minimize any language, gestures, or tone of voice that communicates harshness or disrespect.	Using a loud voice, pointing, throwing, punching, blaming, or accusing.
Start with an "I notice..." statement and then state clearly and succinctly what isn't working for you.	Using phrases such as "you always" and "you never"; being vague or ambiguous or overly complex.

For example:
    While the two of you are enjoying a walk together, in a calm voice you say:

"I notice that when you change your clothes at night, you throw them on the floor and don't pick them up, even the following day."

Then give a statement about how this makes you FEEL:

"The mess makes me feel like you don't respect our space. I also feel taken advantage of because you expect me to do something you're capable of doing yourself."

Then you can ask him/her for what you want, simply and calmly, including a measure of time for change. When you state your request, be sure to identify the specific behavior you want changed.

"I don't want to live in a messy environment or have to pick up after you. I'd like you to put your dirty clothes in the hamper when you take them off."

Then discuss it. Listen to his/her side. Make whatever adjustments or compromises need to be made. When you reach a clear agreement, each person states it clearly and concisely.

"Okay, I will pick up all my clothes every morning before I leave for work."

"Agreed. You will pick up your clothes every morning before you go to work."

That wasn't so bad, was it? When you put these guidelines to use in approaching any potentially difficult conversations, I'm sure you'll find your way through it with much greater ease.

"Why can't you just accept me the way I am?" is a frequent response when someone is asked to change. What this means is "Why can't you love me unconditionally?" Of course, we would like to love others unconditionally, but we have needs and we have conditions. That's a simple fact.

Sometimes people ask, "Why can't you just accept me the way I am?" as a defense for not wanting to take on responsibility or because they don't want to give up a destructive habit. It's easy to get snagged by that one. Be cautious. You have a right to your needs and desires.

Another frequently used defense is accusing the person asking for change of being "controlling." Again, be cautious of their motivation. Are you trying to control them, or are they trying to get out of upholding their agreements or their responsibilities? People don't like to feel they have a dictator running their lives. So, to avoid this being a reality, watch your attitude, tone of voice, and manner in which you request the changes you want/need. The chart on page 85 will help with that.

Sometimes it's difficult to tell when words and attitudes are meant to support another person and when they (consciously or unconsciously) are meant to control another. A controlling voice sounds like this: "Let me do that for you." "Do it now or you're in big trouble." "Stop doing that." "You want this one, not that one."

A supportive voice sounds like this: "Can I assist

you?" "These bills are almost overdue. Can you have the checks written and ready to mail by this evening?" "What you're doing is really annoying me. Could you please stop." "I like this one. Which one do you want?"

When you want to support others in changing their behaviors, give them choices and empower them to take responsibility for their actions. When you ask someone to choose, you honor him or her as individuals. It's a way of saying, "I respect you." When people feel respected, they are much more inclined to align with you or your point of view. Conversely, when they feel controlled, dominated, or insignificant, they are less apt to co-operate.

So be BIG and be kind. Empower others by giving them choices and watch their behaviors evolve!

When your needs are *not* being met, it is far more loving to let the other person know about it than hide it inside, along with a grudge. Nobody knows exactly what you need except you. Family members, friends, and business associates can't read your mind. **Appropriately acknowledging your needs to others is an act of self-love and serves the relationship in many ways.**

> My buddy Rob had a wife who frequently bounced checks. This really upset him. One day, he decided that instead of raging to himself about it, he would explain his feelings and ask her to stop bouncing checks.

Following the step-by-step process on page 85, Rob told his wife how upset her bad habit made him. It wasn't difficult for her to see why he was so mad. Cherishing the relationship, she called on her support system to help her work out the overspending. In time, she was able to overcome the problem and the relationship remained a harmonious and happy one.

Had Rob not asked her to change, it's likely his resentment and anger would have poisoned their relationship, breaking essential ties and connections. You can see that asking your partner, teenagers, or business associates to alter their bad habits or to meet your needs can be an essential ingredient for a healthy, long-lasting relationship. So, be aware of what doesn't feel right, and speak up about needs that are not being met.

When working this out, negotiation is important. Talk back and forth so both parties' feelings can be heard and their needs can get met. You may find it helpful to review the "understanding" and "active listening" processes at the end of the section on *Healthy Thoughts* on pages 16-19 before going into a negotiation.

Negotiating so your needs are met is necessary in every relationship. No two partners know everything about the other's needs or sensitivities. By communicating about your needs and desires through calm and clear conversation, you can resolve most issues. Be willing to honor whatever your partners say about their needs.

Negotiating is like two people putting their "cards" on the table, respectfully listening, and calmly responding to one another. Think of how businessmen negotiate. They go back and forth in a manner of acceptance until some resolve has been determined. Then they make a clear agreement, most often writing it down, and keeping to its terms.

Do the same in your personal relationships by keeping a cool head, speaking clearly and diplomatically, and respecting your partners' feelings, needs, and wants. Let them know you understand them, and spell out what they can expect from you.

Now, when the people you ask to change their behavior actually *do* change, be sure to acknowledge their progress and congratulate them! If they slip back, remember, new habits don't form overnight. They take time. Remind them gently. Praise their efforts and cheer them on to victory!

Asking someone to change can be a gesture of love. It can be the impetus for healing, which can lead to greater closeness, instead of greater separation. So WALK TALL, and when it doesn't feel good, ask the person to change.

5. If the person doesn't change, create distance. Sometimes you ask people to change and they won't. Or they say they will but don't. In such cases, it's time to create some distance.

Creating distance from friends and associates is not

too hard. We just stop spending so much time togeth-er—on the phone, at the gym, at parties, studying, whatever. We can shift to spending time with other peo-ple or spending more time alone. We can find things to do outside the existing circle of friends. We can stop calling them. We can say no when they invite us some-where. We can stop being so chummy. Creating distance can be a fabulous survival tool for any relationship.

With people who live in the same household, though, creating distance becomes more challenging. By sheer proximity, we are "close." In such cases, we can create distance by withdrawing emotionally or otherwise.

When couples wrestle with a difficulty or conflict that cannot be resolved, and distance begins to grow between the partners, I strongly suggest seeking pro-fessional council. An experienced therapist, coach, or social worker can facilitate couples in breaking through the barriers of communication. A professional can support a couple in learning new ways to commu-nicate, opening up the flow of affection again, and moving towards both people getting their needs met.

Creating distance with people you don't feel good being around can be the way to re-establish harmony, peace, and love. Though this action may change the *form* of the relationship, it will allow it to live on and on.

Here's a situation in which creating distance made a big difference:

One night **many** moons ago, after dancing in
a club in Santa Monica with a bunch of friends, I

was walking to my car. We passed by a good-looking guy leaning up against a parking meter. He was squatting, so our eyes were at the same level. He wore a black leather jacket and greeted me with smiling eyes. I saw a motorcycle behind him. As I passed by, I teasingly said, "Take me for a ride?" My friends grabbed me by the back of my collar and escorted me to my car.

A few weeks later, I was in that same club with my friend Eeo. I had told her about the handsome motorcycle man with the sparkly eyes. Eeo and I were dancing away, having a great time. I looked up at Eeo and she was pointing at someone, saying to me, "Check out that guy!!" I looked over and, believe it or not, it was that motorcycle man, in his black leather jacket! I said, "That's him!!" Fergy happened to be walking over to ask Eeo to dance, and then he saw me. That was it. For the next chapter of life, the three of us were a trio.

Fergy eventually became my crush, then my beau. He was a free spirit, that Fergy-dog. At first I found that "free-sprit" thing very attractive. After a while however, I grew very uncomfortable with not knowing where he was or when I might see him again. Through all the worry and stress I developed an ulcer.

As you might imagine, my demands made him

uncomfortable. So, we made more distance in the relationship. It actually turned out to be a great thing because we broke up before things got nasty and mean. We parted as friends, acknowledging each others needs and have remained friends over all these years. He called me just last week to wish me happy birthday. I was thrilled to talk to my old pal Fergy. I hope our friendship lasts until the twilight hours of our lives.

We've all had relationships that didn't work out. When we step back and get a little more distance, many times the friendship is easy, wonderful, and right. Sometimes taking a step back is a way to make a beautiful thing last for a very long time.

SAY NO TO WHAT YOU DON'T WANT

I always say, "The more you say no to what you don't want, the more the universe gives you what you do want."

It was July 1st a few summers ago. I got in my car and drove from my home in Boulder to downtown Denver. Walking into the Marriott Hotel, I was delighted to find a set of stairs in front of the check-in desk. So I climbed up, looked the clerk in the eye and gave my signature with no trouble at all. Turning around, I saw the room

LP friends

was full of Little People. It was the 38th annual Little People of America's national convention.

At the time of that convention, I was 40 and still had never been married. Since my early 20s, I had wanted to be married, but it just never worked out. I had a knack for gravitating toward men who were unavailable in one way or another. Simply stated, my history with romantic relationships was abominable. But, at this point in time, I was feeling darn good about myself and walking quite tall. I felt ready to meet my man!

The first evening there, I met a really cute guy from England named Dale. Blond, easy to talk to, I felt attracted to him right away. We spent much time enjoying one another's company over the next few days. I learned some great things about this guy, but also some that weren't so great. First, he lived in England. Second, he supposedly had a girlfriend. And, third, one moment he seemed interested in me and the next moment, I wasn't really sure. The most amazing thing, though, was that even with all this information, I felt **compelled** to go for it. Something about him seemed so attractive, so familiar.

About half way through the convention week, I met another really cute guy named Brad, from Milwaukee. Brad had long thick hair and the most amazing eyelashes I'd ever seen. In our brief conversations through one evening, I noticed how incredibly sweet he was and how good I felt receiving his pointed attention.

At about 1:00 a.m. when the convention dance was over, I found myself sitting in the hotel lobby, Dale in the chair to my right and Brad in the chair to my left. Whoa! How to play this hand? I wondered. Carefully, tenuously...I began to engage them both simultaneously.

In the midst of this intensely awkward situation, I noticed Dale's attention bouncing around the room like a tennis ball. Brad, however, focused on me like a laser beam. Still, I kept feeling this magnetic pull toward Dale. And when I looked over at Brad, the feelings of excitement just weren't there.

After a while, Dale said he was going upstairs to a party—without expressing much concern for me. I pretended I didn't notice and popped up out of my chair to follow him. As Dale walked away, I turned to Brad and said something lame like, "I think I'll be right back."

What was I going to do? Scuffling across the marble floor toward the elevator, I had no clue about what to do next. Then the elevator door opened and Dale stepped in. I looked at him. I felt drawn to him as a moth to a flame. My insides ached. Just then, I heard a voice inside as if it came over a loud speaker. "You can step into that elevator and do what you've always done. Or you can go over there and do something new."

"Hi-Ho Silver!" It was my superhero, my inner guide! The message was clear. I mustered up restraint in every muscle. I held myself back from taking that step. The doors closed an inch from my face. There I was. I had done it! I had said no to what I did not want.

Sometimes it's difficult to say no. Sometimes we feel attracted toward people because they're familiar, and not necessarily because they are healthy for us. I let the universe know I didn't want any more relationships with unavailable men, not just through my prayers but through my actions, through my *choices*. Then something amazing happened.

About four days later, I was having breakfast with Brad. We had spent a lot of time together over that convention week. Bubbles of fresh love were flowing, to say the least. He reached across the table and took my hand. He gave me this ominous look. I didn't know what he was going to say.

Then, with a gentle voice, he said, "Honey, you are my destiny. You're the only woman for me. I know we'll always be together."

I'd been waiting for mutual love for a very long time. And here it was. As real as a red fire engine.

A year later, our families and friends gathered in my folks' yard. It was a perfect summer day (which, in Cleveland, is a rare occurrence). The evening sun set everything aglow. Standing beneath a willow arch, laced with white roses, we said our vows and exchanged our rings. There we stood: Mr. and Mrs. Bradley Laise.

As a special treat, the minister asked everyone to open the little white boxes placed beneath their seats. Butterflies fluttered out and filled the air.

Oh happy day!

See! It really is true. The more you say no to what you don't want, the more the universe delivers what you do want!

Not long ago, I was reading a book by Suze Orman on fulfilling your financial dreams. In the beginning of the book, she talked about healthy habits for creating more wealth and abundance. She prescribed going through the entire house—every cupboard, drawer, closet, and storage space—and pulling out everything you no longer use or do not want. Then she suggested that these things be sold or given away as soon as possible.

This exercise is based on the principle of saying "no" to what you *do not* want, so you can make space for what you *do* want. When there's room for something new, then the universe can give it to us. If there is no void, then there is no need to fill.

The same principle applies to our emotional lives: the more we let go of relationships that don't give us what we want, the more space we make to receive the kind of relationships we *do* want.

People often talk about holding on to a relationship with a person who *used to* give them so much love but was no longer interested. This "holding on" sometimes goes on for months, and even years. It reminds me of a story that my meditation teacher, Maharishi, used to tell.

Once there was a boy named Keva who was born in a hut. The hut was all Keva knew. He grew up there, got married there, and raised his kids there.

One day, Keva was invited by his master to join him living in the palace. He was so excited! He packed up his family and hurried into his new home of grandeur.

But soon Keva became very uncomfortable living in the palace. The marble floors were cold, the painted walls distracting. Keva's discomfort grew, and soon he moved with his family back to the hut. There he felt comfortable again.

When we get used to something, sometimes it's difficult to let go of it and expand, to open to more abundance. Letting go of what we do not want can be difficult. But letting go allows us to receive all the wonders of the universe.

❽

HEALTHY
LIFE

CREATE THE LIFE YOU REALLY WANT

If you know that...

> you create your life
> through your choices,

+   you have the power
to choose what you want

> you can live the life you've
> always dreamed of

> "
> *Go confidently in*
> *the direction of*
> *your dreams!*
> *Live the life*
> *you've imagined.*
> "
>
> —HENRY DAVID
> THOREAU

...why not make it happen?

Here are eleven tips to help you go from where you
are to where you want to be:

1. Know that you are co-creating The foundation of
creating the life you want is fully understanding and
accepting that you and God *together* are creating this

thing called "your life." It's not one or the other; it's both.

2. Dream BIG! Expand your limits. Dream bigger than you have ever dreamed before! Let your imagination burst open and get HUGE! Let your desire fill up with all the things you would love to know, see, feel, do, and be! Let your vision encompass the grandest ideals, the most spectacular notions, and the highest truths. Let your dreams be bigger than life. Because *anything* is possible.

3. Clarify your values What's important to you? This is the question to help get clear on what you truly value. What people, things, places, events, etc., in your life are most meaningful and significant? Carefully look inside and see what's true for you.

Make a list of these things. Prioritize them by giving each item a rating 1-10, 10 being highest. What's the *most* important thing on your list, what's the least important? Be true to your *own* heart, setting aside the values of others (like your parents' or spouse's). This list is your own unique set of values and ideals. This is to help you clarify what is most important to *you.*

Take good care of this piece of paper as it holds vital information that will steer your actions, like a rudder steers a boat. What is important to you determines what you do, how you spend your time, what choices you make. Get clear on what you value most so you know when to turn right and when to turn left. Update your list of values as they change.

4. Get clear on what you want Ask yourself, "Where do I want to be in five years? Ten years? Twenty years? What kind of work do I want to be doing? Where do I want to be living? How do I want to be living, and with whom?" Finally, ask yourself, "What do I really want now and in the future?"

A great exercise to gain deeper clarity on this topic is to imagine your ideal day. Take a few minutes to lie down and close your eyes. After taking a couple of deep breaths, begin imagining your ideal day, starting from the moment you wake up to the moment you go to sleep. Imagine all the details of your day—surroundings, activities, relationships—just the way you would like them to be. What do you do, eat, and wear? How does it all look, feel, and taste? Visualize at a deep level and make it as close to your ideal as possible.

When you sit up, jot down what you have just learned about yourself. Let yourself see how you would really like things to be. Then use this sheet to steer that boat called your life.

5. Design a plan Now that you know what's important to you and what you truly want, it's time to create a plan that takes you from where you are to where you want to be.

So, *brainstorm*. Jot down all the ideas, plans, schemes, and strategies that you can possibly think of. Write whatever comes to mind. Think BIG! Include in your list all the resources you have available to you: your skills, your contacts, your friends, relatives, coaches, people who will help you. Also include your strengths and weaknesses.

Now organize all your ideas into a solid and powerful plan. Your plan can be simple or complex. It can be one step or several steps. Your plan is like a blueprint. The closer the blueprint maps out your final vision, the closer you will end up where you want to be.

6. Set goals and time lines With a plan in hand, you can begin setting specific goals and assigning time lines to each. Write them. Chart your time. Post your plan somewhere where you can see it often. Review it weekly or bi-weekly and make adjustments as needed. Check off the goals you have accomplished. Most importantly, be sure to acknowledge yourself for your accomplishments.

7. Make goals realistic The best way to get frustrated, disappointed, and discouraged is to expect too much too soon. When looking at your goals, make sure they are truly feasible within a reasonable time frame. People who set goals like, "I'm going to lose fifty pounds in the next *two* weeks!" are only setting themselves up for failure. This kind of thinking gives birth to inner smallness.

Think BIG, but plan realistically.

8. Gather support Sometimes you don't have a clue how to achieve the difficult thing you want to achieve. Sometimes you need guidance. If that's the case, find a good teacher, coach, or mentor. Maybe you need a good therapist. The world is full of people who would love to help you. Some will charge you money; some will do it by virtue of goodwill. Whatever your resources, find someone who is excellent at what they do, strives for excellence themselves, and believes in you. Remember, asking for help is good.

9. Get back up on the horse When you fall off a horse, the best thing to do is to get back on it and continue riding. This helps overcome the fear instilled through the fall. When you meet with failure, you must remember that victory is in the *process*. Get back up and ride on!

10. Be accountable The more you do what you say you'll do, keep your agreements, and fulfill your responsibilities, the more people will trust you. Being trustworthy is a central trait of people who WALK TALL.

Many times, people think that once they have made an agreement with someone, they must honor it to uphold their sense of integrity. However, things change and sometimes a new agreement needs to be negotiated. So, do that and communicate with those who it will affect. Let them know what they can or cannot expect from you. This way, you allow life to happen and maintain your accountability at the same time.

11. Match your values and your life Is what you value most getting the heart of your attention? Do you give the majority of your time and commitment to the thing(s) you value most? Or is there a discrepancy between what you value and how you spend your time and resources?

Do you need to make some adjustments to get the "boat" of your life going in the direction you really want to go? If so, do so. If you match your life with what's important to you, WALKING TALL will be a natural outcome.

PART ONE
CONCLUSION

> "
> *Love your life,*
> *perfect your life,*
> *beautify all things*
> *in your life.*
> "
>
> —TECUMSEH,
> CHIEF OF THE
> SHAWNEE NATION

We can learn an enormous amount about how to improve our lives. But nothing will ever get better until we start making different choices.

Your moment-to-moment choices about what to think, say, and do all create the thing called "your life." So, to make it better, make healthier choices.

Making different choices requires you to stretch! It also supports you in getting BIG on the INside as well. Making healthy choices brings forth positive experiences and nourishes your well being. So—Be BIG! WALK TALL, and choose what's healthy on all levels, in all ways.

PART TWO

....

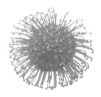

DOING
THE
MONSTER
DANCE

INTRO:
BIG BOYS
DON'T CRY

....

While growing up, many of us frequently received the message "big boys don't cry," and "nice girls don't get angry." That taught us to avoid at all costs feelings that we labeled as "negative." If we didn't, who knew what might happen? We might hurt someone. We might shrivel up from the anguish and die. We might lose control and do something crazy. We might make fools of ourselves! What monster might emerge if we took even the slightest step in that direction?

In recent times, however, teachers, therapists, and even spiritual schools are reexamining the old cultural trends and attitudes toward emotions, showing us there is more to the business of emotions than we had ever imagined.

❶

E-MOTIONS

ALLOW THOSE ENERGIES TO MOVE

One day when I was about 28, I was confiding in my best friend, Eeo. Tears ran down my face from another rejection, another heartbreak. My friend responded with tender compassion, as she did so frequently. She rubbed my back and, with a soft voice, said, "Why not join me and come to Anna's dance class?"

I stared at my friend, bewildered. I knew Anna's dance class was not an evening dance class, not a weekend workshop, nor a week long retreat. This dance class was every day, five days a week, for almost an entire year!

I glanced up at my friend. I glanced down at myself. I said, "Me a dancer? **I don't think so!**"

"Anna is no **ordinary** dancer," my friend

explained. "She celebrates differences! Anna dances and works with people who are crippled, overweight, and challenged to beat cancer. Her passion is to work with people who are different. It'll be great, I promise!" Now, let it be known that Eeo could sell ice to an Eskimo. Eventually, she won me over.

Amazing! That was my first impression of Anna Halprin. Though Anna was 62 years old when I met her, her movements were as fluid as rain. Even more impressive, Anna had had her colon removed while battling cancer during her early 50s. That didn't hold her back in the least, however. She still danced every day, taught in her school, ran her business, and traveled the globe to bring her work to people in distant lands. It was clear from the get-go that Anna was blessed with a gigantic spirit. She was a triumphant warrior, ablaze with creativity and an overflowing zest for life.

The first day of class, I woke up feeling apprehensive. I wasn't really sure what we were going to do in Anna's beautiful studio. I knew we wouldn't be doing pirouettes and pliés. This wasn't ballet. And I knew we wouldn't be doing up-up-downs. Anna wasn't a modern dancer. So what would we be doing there, I pondered?

Each week, Anna revealed new movement explorations. We learned something different every day, and mostly things I had never experienced before.

We'd begin a typical day at the studio with "movement ritual," which was Anna's unique concoction of yoga poses. On the heated wooden floor we would bend, stretch, and breathe in a series of postures that flowed in slow motion. Because of my short limbs, I had difficulty performing the poses. But contrary to any prior athletic endeavor I'd done, my lack of precision didn't really matter. "Approximate" was good enough for Anna. Yet amidst the accepting external environment, I struggled inside as I compared myself to the others with their long limbs and perfect postures.

Throughout the day, we did lots of interactive exercises and movements, many times in groups. Often we worked closely, body to body. I didn't fit any of the other bodies; that made me feel really uncomfortable. Many times we were asked to move around the studio shoulder-to-shoulder, back-to-back, head-to-head. These exercises and dances always brought up an overpowering sense of inadequacy inside me. Need I say the time I spent in that studio pushed my buttons?

To make matters worse, Anna's daughter Daria came to teach one day a week. Her job was to stir up psychological material for us to work with. For example, she'd have us reflect on the burden we carried in the world, or on difficult moments we'd had with each of our parents. Then she'd ask us to express those impressions through movement.

Before long, it became apparent this dance class wasn't really about "dance" as I had ever understood the word to mean. No. This class was about coming to terms with myself.

Here I was—living in a state distant from my home, doing things completely foreign to me, and stuck in the middle of what felt like a perpetual "encounter group." My family's belief about psychological therapy was that if you needed it you were crazy, a nut, a bona fide lunatic. In short, we believed that ignoring problems made them go away. So, what the heck was I doing **there**?

Despite my agitation, I continued to go to the studio day after day. Anna magnificently did her part to accept me as I was. She truly celebrated my differences. It was clear at this point who was the bigger person between us. I bit my upper lip and did my best not to show anyone the feelings churning inside me like a volcano ready to explode.

Over time, Anna gave me a new perspective on just about everything; about seeing differences as a good thing, accepting limitations, and, of course, expressing emotions.

Anna said, "Emotions," and she wrote E-motions, "are energies in motion, energies that must move! We human beings have a whole range of energies like joy, anger, love, and sadness that must move. It's not a problem for us to let pleasant emotions like joy and love move freely. But when it comes to those nasty, ugly emotions like anger, jealousy, and sadness, it's not so easy because of their discomfort and disruptive natures. So we tend to push them away, hiding them deep down inside of us."

After that class, I began to take notice of my difficult feelings rising up. I also started to notice myself pushing them back down automatically, just as I had always done, just as she had described.

One winter day, Anna asked me to do a movement, one I felt I couldn't do as well as the others. I told her I didn't want to do it. "Peggy," she said with a blast of her warrior spirit, "I think it's time for you to do the Monster Dance!" I looked up at her and said, "What? What's the Monster Dance?"

"Remember, we talked last week about pent-up negative emotions? Your monster is all those ugly emotions you hold inside and don't let anyone see. Doing the Monster Dance lets that monster OUT and frees us from its negative influence. So, go ahead Peggy. Take what you're feeling right now and express it in movement."

The theory sounded good, but there was no way I was going to do any "Monster" Dance in front of the entire group, that was for sure.

"Come on," she encouraged.

I realized I couldn't get out of this. So, reluctantly, I raised my hands above my head and contracted all the muscles in my face. In a slightly raised voice, I said, "Stop laughing at me. Stop it!"

"Not bad for first try." Anna said. "But this time, really feel your anger and yell it out!"

Because I felt so embarrassed by my first go at it, the thought of doing it again made me feel like throwing up. "Go for it!" she shouted, as if to show me how to use my voice.

I closed my eyes and imagined those kids on the playground who used to always laugh at me. My fists and face began to clench. "Stop!" I hollered. "Stop it! Go away!"

I thought I had passed the test, but not so. Anna got down on her hands and knees. She howled and growled furiously as she rose up mimicing the movements of a gigantic bear.

"I want you to give it all you've got this time. Let 'er rip!" she yelled.

Again? I have to do this idiotic thing again? I quibbled inside.

I closed my eyes once more and revisited those

kids calling me names, pushing me down, and laughing at me. I let myself begin to feel what I had been holding inside for over 20 years: RAGE— "YYYAAAHHH!" I screamed from the bottom of my gut. "I hate you! I hate you! Get away from me! Leave me alone!"

I jumped back. I couldn't believe what had just come out of me. I couldn't believe my huge voice, my enormous intensity, and my gargantuan power! I opened my eyes and looked down at my body. I couldn't believe I was still only 42 inches because I felt like I was **10 feet tall!**

Thus began my reconciliation with the myth that feeling so-called negative emotions are a bad thing, and that "nice girls don't get angry." Thus began my growing appreciation for the invaluable gifts that arise out of letting these emotions move in appropriate ways.

I later came to learn that Anna invented the Monster Dance in the hospital while she was recovering from cancer. She began rolling around in her bed, dancing, giving permission to her difficult emotions to move through her without hurting herself or anyone else. She then experimented with other forms of expressive art like writing, drawing, and making music. In her training, we used all these modalities, and more, to transform our ugly emotions into something beautiful and potent: art.

We wrote stories about our monsters and shared them with our classmates. We drew pictures with large crayons in bold colors of our pent-up anger, frustration, and rage. Some of the monster drawings looked like this:

We made masks of our monsters, put them on, and danced the persona of our dark side. In each exercise, I felt a growing sense of strength and power. I felt supported from within by my own courage. A natural sense of confidence began to blossom inside. **I now felt equipped to deal with the difficulties of my everyday life.**

I left Anna's with many blessings. No price can even come close to how valuable these awakenings have been to me.

(For more information on Anna Halprin's work, refer to the Suggested Resource List.)

❷

WHAT TREASURES
LIE BENEATH

Everyone has a treasure inside. Some experience this treasure as a gold chest lined with shimmering gems, overflowing with diamonds, strings of pearls, sparkling rubies, and glistening precious coins. Others sense their inner treasure as an infinite ocean of love, an enormous diamond, or as a fountain of vitality and joy. People may experience their

> "
> *If the doors of perception were cleansed, everything would appear to man as it is, infinite.*
> "
>
> —WILLIAM BLAKE

inner treasure in a variety of metaphorical images. Yet they all represent the truth: that unlimited goodness, value, creativity, power, compassion, wisdom, and strength all dwell deep inside of us.

If you don't regularly experience this treasure within, you may have lost connection to your inner self. This happens when your windows of perception become dirty, or when your internal "stuff" blocks the way. As a result, you don't feel precious or truly fulfilled, In fact, you may feel empty, even worthless. Thus, you attempt to win the favor of others so they can remind you of your value. Gaining this external validation can be exhausting as well as disappointing.

As doing the Monster Dance with Anna illustrates, giving permission to move ugly repressed emotions is one very effective technique to clean the windows of perception. It can help reestablish a connection with the positive resources hidden inside. Frozen emotions can block you from that treasure; flowing emotions can open many doors.

VIEW EMOTIONS AS A DOORWAY

In the section "Find the Gift Inside the Challenge," we talked about how pain can be a doorway into expansion and transformation, how it can be an invitation to grow. And if we walk through that doorway, we may discover gifts, the treasure that lies deep within.

When Anna asked me to do the Monster Dance, she handed me an invitation to the "party of life," to meet my pain and be transformed by it. In doing so, I grew in many ways. I found many benefits to facing emotional pain by creatively expressing and releasing it. I learned:

• I could transform something negative into something positive.

• The healing power inherent in accepting something I had been rejecting.

• That repressing my anger left me feeling weak and victimized.
• That letting my anger move, express, and release reconnected me with my innate strength and courage.
• That I am not small and helpless, but actually I am HUGE and powerful!

This appreciation grew deeper several years later while I was studying a body-centered psychotherapy called Hakomi. (Hakomi is a Hopi Indian word that means, "Who am I?") As I went on to become a certified Hakomi therapist, working with my clients, I witnessed these principles of self-empowerment being realized repeatedly and consistently.

In Hakomi, we direct people to what's going inside so they can study their body-mind-spirit connection in a gentle, nonviolent and organic manner. This leads to clarity about how they hold themselves back and to the truth of who they are. In my work as a psychotherapist, I found many other forms of doing the monster dance, techniques like Hakomi, that facilitate opening the door of emotional difficulty and revealing many gifts beneath the surface.

These practices hold immense value if they are approached not for the drama, but for the understandings that arise out of the release, and for the cleansing of the windows of perception they provide. The techniques described in this upcoming section are more therapeutic than artistic in nature. Let's look at two variations on the Monster Dance: Expressing and Releasing, and Following the Thread.

Expressing and Releasing Expressing and Releasing can be as direct as a lightning bolt. This form of the Monster Dance allows anger to get expressed through assertive movements like hitting and punching (pillows, of course, never people).

Expressing and releasing usually manages emotions like anger, frustration, and fear. You can express and release ugly emotions safely in a variety of ways. The section *Go For It!* outlines several techniques in detail, walking you through the "how to" process step by step.

Practicing these techniques, you'll most likely notice a surge of energy and power through your entire body. When you rest afterwards, you'll probably experience an incredible clarity of mind. Confusion often gets erased. By focusing your attention on the expansion in your body and mind, it's common to experience an expansion of mind so profound that you have deep insights into your psyche. Often you'll gain an understanding of things that have always puzzled you— things like how you hold yourself back or why you overreact in certain situations.

Once you understand these things about yourself, you then have the power and freedom to start changing them.

One day when I was in my mid-30s, a few years after leaving Anna's, I was feeling extremely upset and angry about a failed relationship. I had had it! I was fed up with that pain and never wanted to feel it again. I decided to go to the pillows and let myself express and release my real feelings about it. So, I piled up some big pillows and got out my bat.

I started breathing deeply to get the energy moving. I focused on my emotions, getting present with my anger and rage. I bashed the pillows as hard as I could with my bat and shouted again and again. I expressed my anger at God for giving me a body that others didn't see as valuable. I let my rage roar as I thought of the many people in my life who found it impossible to love me fully. This went on for 15 or 20 minutes; my anger and rage just kept flooding out of me.

I stopped, lay down, closed my eyes, and noticed how deeply I was breathing. I felt HUGE inside, alive and awake! My mind was as clear as a bright blue sky. Words rose up inside of me with power and clarity. "I'm the one who doesn't see my value, but I blame it on God and everyone else." Then I realized: **It's because I believe I am nothing that love passes me by.**

A light had turned on inside. I could see how my unconscious beliefs had been working against me. I could see that it wasn't necessarily others who didn't see my value. It was **me.** I understood then that if I took responsibility for accepting and loving myself, things would most *likely change. From that day on I did my best to see my own value and not blame others. It took years to develop the ability to stop blaming others, but once I did, life became much sweeter.*

This is how letting out the monster—the pent-up rage—can transform negativity into positivity. This is how expressing and releasing our authentic emotions can clean us out so we can see things more clearly, more objectively. This is how fully entering into the emotions can be a doorway to truth and freedom.

Following the Thread "Expressing and Releasing" uses big movements, *macro*-movements. Sometimes that works great. At other times, it's better to process challenging emotions by going to the other end of the spectrum through *micro*-movements.

This process requires staying alert and being present with whatever is happening and with whatever arises in the moment. While sitting comfortably, with eyes closed, we focus on what is happening inside of us right here and right now. We follow the thread of our inner experience as it changes and unfolds. As we do, it takes us deeper.

Many times we come to a place of challenge, a place where what is present is very uncomfortable—perhaps a place of terror or worthlessness. These feelings are difficult to tolerate, but as we grow in our ability to stay present through them, we come out the other side, to an open place, an expansive state.

Here's an excerpt from my journal from an evening when I was feeling sad and so decided to use the "Follow the Thread" technique.

I had just finished a difficult conversation with a friend and hung up the phone feeling sad. I went to my room and sat on my bed. After I took a few breaths, the feeling of sadness began to deepen. My attention was drawn to an ache in my chest. Placing my focus there, it felt like a knife was dragging down the center of my chest. Tears streamed across the sides of my face. Enduring these difficulties, I noticed that underneath the sadness was a belief of being not good enough. It felt very familiar, as old as my years on Earth. It seemed as though I was never enough for anyone, not even my parents. I noticed how I was always trying to make up for that, putting forth so much effort in my relationships, hoping to be worthy of love.

I continued to breathe deeply and followed what was arising next. It was a longing, a deep longing for myself—to uncover it, to discover it, to know it, to be it. Then I saw myself in a vast desert, searching and calling out for my **real** self—my natural self—without all the trying. I wandered long and far in the search.

Then I saw my true self! It appeared as a Christmas tree with sparkling white lights, trimmed with candy and beautiful sparkly things.

I knew this was a representation of a deeper part of me that had been covered up. I called it a "living treasure." Then I noticed compassion—compassion for the part of me that believed I had to work to get love. The compassion was soothing and gentle. It spread over my whole body and I felt profoundly relaxed. I felt the presence of a tender love.

TRANSFORM EMOTIONS INTO ESSENCE

As you practice the Monster Dance in whatever form suits you best, you'll likely find many emotions in the anger family pent up inside, like rage, hatred, and frustration. You will probably notice constellations of feelings from the sad family: hurt, grief, heartache. And some more from the fear family: anxiety, worry, panic, terror. Then there are also the neighbors of fear: helplessness, powerlessness, and valuelessness. The range of emotions is enormous. But the amazing thing is, beneath each one lies an incredible gift.

When you focus on and let your anger move through you, "essential" *strength* naturally arises inside—clarity of mind, creativity, aliveness, and courage, too. When you let yourself feel your sadness in an authentic way—not in a pity-pot sort of way, but really allowing yourself to feel it—it will give rise to "essential" *compassion,* soft, gentle healing. This love—for yourself and others—is the central force that heals all.

When we let our emotions move, it is not easy at first to see what is behind them. We are not used to seeing, sensing, or feeling these subtle forces. To locate them most easily, ask self-directed questions such as, "What do I feel in my body right now, in my chest, my legs, my head? Is there a change from before? If so, what is it?" Then really tune in and sense the answers with your heart.

Some people will notice these subtle qualities right away. For others, it takes more time. Be patient. People perceive essence in different ways. Some see images inside—beautiful, touching. Some hear tones or songs. Some taste flavors or smell aromas related to the expansive experience currently taking place.

Sometimes people don't seem to make it all the way through to the expansive state. Nothing much seems to transform. They feel stuck. That's okay. That's normal. It takes time and focus to break through. It doesn't happen overnight. I spent years developing an inner life and exploring my emotions before things started to shift in a significant way. So, if you feel stuck— have faith, persist, and if you want or need help from a professional, find it.

A common place to get stuck is in fear. Fear is difficult to stay with and move through because you often feel as though you are going to die. It helps to understand that what actually dies is the old way of being, the old way of doing and reacting.

With fear, helplessness, powerlessness, and valueless-ness, we often come to a deep inner experience of a black hole. It's like we are in a cavern of pure blackness that swallows us. Because facing this can be challenging, we can be greatly assisted by working with a therapist or spiritual teacher who knows about black holes and how to work through them. I strongly recommend getting professional support for this, or for any part of process-ing your emotions—especially if you feel stuck or are serious about breaking free toward a significantly new level of freedom.

Once you build enough trust in your process, you will be able to endure black holes. When you go into it and pass through it, you'll see it transforms into peace—peace so deep you cannot shake it.

Here's an excerpt from a session I did several years ago with my teacher Morton:

> I began the session telling Morton how shaky things had been with my boyfriend Adam. He asked me how I was feeling in my body. I replied, "My stomach is churning and very upset. I feel afraid I'm going to blow it with him. I really want this relationship to work out. Under the fear I feel helpless, as if I have absolutely no control over what might happen between us."
>
> Morton asked me to turn my gaze inward and go deeper. I saw a hole in my chest—a black hole—as big as a sewer pipe going into the black

forever. Morton suggested I go in the hole and see what's in there. I said, "No way! It will swallow me alive." He said, "Do you know that for sure?" I said, "No." "Then why not find out for yourself," he said convincingly. So I went into the hole. Deep pain of being **nothing** came up and filled me. As I tolerated the feeling, the pain deepened with a sense of shame. With the shame came an awareness that what I show to the world is all a false fabrication. Tears flowed.

Morton asked me, "What is happening now?"

After a few moments of feeling the shame, it began to subside and I felt peace. The peace expanded and deepened and I felt my body let go of all its tension. The peace seemed to go on forever. I noticed then a deep acceptance for myself, for my body, and for whatever would happen next.

These are the treasures that lie within. They have always been there, only they have been covered up.

You see, as babies, we come into this world as whole human beings, completely connected to our inner selves, our spirit. But through the process of growing up, we encounter physical pain, emotional difficulties, and physical traumas. Each time we hold in an emotion, whether to avoid its pain or because we have been taught to do so, we stop the flow of authentic energy.

This break in the energy flow severs the connection to our inner selves, our essence.

It's like a bicycle wheel that has an outer and an inner wheel connected to each other by spokes. When a spoke breaks, the outer wheel loses its connection with the hub, and is weakened. When the spoke is repaired, the wheel becomes whole again, re-establishing its full potential. Similarly, when we allow blocked emotions to flow, we reconnect with our essence, our Being, our spirit, and we can eventually regain our wholeness and access our essential qualities like love, peace and strength.

Routinely holding in specific emotions can disconnect us from related aspects of being, or essence. For example, if we block a lot of anger, we lose connection with our inner strength. If we habitually hold in sadness, we get cut off from our essential compassion and love. Repressed fear leads to insecurity; repressed hatred leads to powerlessness.

However, this can all be reversed simply by letting our emotions move in appropriate and safe ways.

Again, I'd like to emphasize that your expansion can be much more efficient with the support of a professional who has "been there, done that." Whether you go the path alone or get support, the techniques in this book can help. (For more information on gaining support, please refer to Suggested Resource List under Hakomi and/or Ridhwan.)

❸

OUT OF
THE BOX

GO FOR IT!

Now that you've read all of these
incredible things about what can
happen when you express and
release your emotions—especially
the ones you call "ugly"—I bet you
just can't wait to start doing them.

> **"**
> *It takes courage*
> *to grow up*
> *and turn out*
> *to be who we*
> *really are.*
> **"**
>
> —e.e. cummings

Some people call these techniques
"out of the box." They really require
stretching—expanding into a bigger way of being,
thinking, seeing, and doing. I always say, "If you want to
grow, you have to stretch!"

Also, you must do your best to quiet the voice inside
that says, "It's not OK to get angry, even if I'm by myself.
It's not OK to pity myself and feel my sadness." Instead,
put all that "small talk" aside, to let yourself experiment,

and see what is true for you.

It may be that you surprise yourself. You might get started with one of these techniques and totally shock yourself because you are so out there, so outrageous. Go for it! Let yourself see how "out of the box" you can be!

In all these techniques, the purpose is to free pent-up emotions for increasing health of body, mind, and spirit. They are meant for your own personal exploration. The negative energy is not to be directed toward anyone else. Always practice them in a safe environment. That means no one gets yelled at, hit, or punched. No one gets hurt.

Remember that this is not about acting out on other people. This is about processing your own stuff so you can reconnect with the inner resources that have been blocked. Keep it safe. Don't hurt yourself or anyone else.

Some therapists will say that expressing anger in dance or towards pillows causes harm because people start to behave more aggressively and it doesn't really lead to anything positive. I say these people probably have a negative judgement of their own anger, or they have only a superficial understanding of these techniques. I suspect they have never felt or looked deep enough inside to see what is there once the energy has moved. Many people, even therapists, overlook the after effect, which is reconnecting to your inner goodness and capacities. Remember, the purpose of this whole section: getting to the treasure beneath all the garbage.

My experience, both in my own personal process, and with many clients has been that just as the body needs to eliminate physical waste, so do we need to eliminate emotional trash. The more we are able to release our negative judgements about difficult emotions, and let them move and express themselves in appropriate ways, the more we can heal. Judging against what exists only creates more suffering. Acceptance is the force that heals.

Many people believe that any form of expressing negativity brings harm. What actually brings harm is when our frustrations, anger, and terror are repressed for so long, we eventually lose control of them and they spill out onto others. The harm can be either aggressive or passive; nonetheless, harm is done.

The practices described here allow the body, mind, and spirit to be cleansed of negativity, to be vital, alive, and whole. They enlarge our capacity for kindness and love, for achievement and success. They lead to real healing.

Here's a detailed description of the many forms of the Monster Dance—creative and dynamic.

FORMS OF THE MONSTER DANCE:
Creative Techniques

E-motions, no matter how ugly you think they are, can flow beautifully through the expressive arts. You can let the monster out of its cage by writing stories about your anger, creating sculpture that expresses your frustration, or writing poems in your journal about your grief or loneliness. You can sing a song, beat a drum, or do a dance that expresses a whole gamut of emotions.

Use any of the expressive arts to let out pent-up emotions and make great art! Drawing, painting, coloring, pastels, charcoal, sculpture—Writing poems, prose, stories, or writing in a stream of consciousness—Playing an instrument, singing a song, beating a drum—Dancing alone, dancing with others, doing the Monster Dance—Computer art, collages, photography... Use all these forms of art, and more, to express, release, and relinquish your monster. Find the one(s) calling to you and go for it!

Afterward, check in with what's going on inside of you. See if there has been a change. Do you feel bigger in any way? More alert or alive? Do you have a sense of freedom or strength or peace? Just look inside quietly, and see.

Therapeutic Techniques

The following techniques are direct and bold. You can do them while you're alone at home, in your bedroom, or even in your car. You may also find it supportive to practice these techniques in groups. Be sure everyone in the circle clearly agrees not to judge or harm one another.

When doing any of the Expressing and Releasing techniques, always use a lot of breath. That means before, during, and after, keep the breath moving at a hearty pace. The breath is like oil that lubricates the machine, getting it ready for movement. So, before letting 'er rip, be sure you're well greased with plenty of oxygen.

As you begin to increase your oxygen intake, start moving your entire body as if you are dancing. You can even wiggle your fingers and toes. As your breath becomes deeper and quicker, be careful not to hyperventilate, of course. If you start feeling light-headed, slow down your breathing. Take it easy for a few moments until you feel centered. Then, start again more slowly.

When you use your voice in a loud fashion, originate the sounds from down in your belly, not up in your throat. If the sounds come from your esophagus area, you're more likely to get a sore throat. If you allow the sound to come from the solar plexus area, you'll feel much more release and power.

Once you express your repressed emotions, you must *release* them. The release part is like flushing the toilet. Wave good-bye, if you wish. But let them go. One of my therapy clients says, "Punch and flush! That's the life for me!"

Dynamic Methods

Here are some therapeutic dynamic methods for transforming your pent-up emotions.

• **The Foot Stomp**—When something really upsets you and you are not in the privacy of your home to process it, do a foot stomp to help pass the anger or frustration through so you don't have to carry it around with you all day long.

Find a private place—a bathroom stall, a car or a place outside. Stand or sit up tall and focus on your upset. Let the emotions emerge and begin taking deeper breaths. Then stomp your feet on the floor or earth as hard and as fast as you can. I don't mean just timidly placing your feet down. I mean really stomping them down! Big! Hard!

When you get tired, stop stomping, but continue taking deep breaths. Then go for another round. Really *feel* the anger and let it out through the stomp. Breathe! Feel the power surge up your legs and into your whole body. How TALL are you walking now?

• **The Hand Scream**—You can do a hand scream just about anywhere, except maybe during a concert or a church sermon. Let your emotions come to the surface. Take a deep breath in and let it out. Put your hand over your mouth and express whatever you are feeling through your muffled scream. Go for it! Let those E-motions roar!

You can use undefined, primitive sounds, or real-life words—words you'd really like to say to whomever upset you. Then feel the release and expansion inside your body. Sense your strength and clarity of mind. Be BIG!

• **The Foot Stomp-Hand Scream Combination**—For a real surge of power, combine these two techniques. Stomp your feet hard as you scream into your hand. This allows a huge release of emotion and a big surge of energy.

• **Screaming Into Pillows**—Take a pillow and hold it up to your mouth. Take a few deep breaths, then scream as loudly as you can into the pillow. The pillow will, of course, muffle the sound.

This is a great exercise for clearing out fear, terror, anger, hatred, frustration, etc. Be sure to breathe a lot and let the sounds come from deep down in your belly. You can make wild sounds, animal-like noises. Or you can shout words and sentences. If you have been abused in any way, this is a perfect opportunity for you to express and release your rage, telling the perpetrator exactly how you feel. Let yourself feel your release and expansion, your strength and your power.

• **Screaming Under Water**—This is the same exercise as screaming in pillows, only you do it when your head is under water. You can holler at the top of your lungs in the bathtub, in the swimming pool, or in the ocean. Water muffles the sound well, so you can really let 'er rip. Also, while you're submerged in the water, it's wonderful to let your body wiggle and waggle freely. Or kick and punch if you like. Don't forget to come up for air!

• **Punching Pillows**—Gather some firm, plain, smooth pillows. They can be pillows from your couch, bed, or cushions. They need to be firm and filled with something that will not emit a lot of dust when they're hit. Old pillows filled with foam are best. Since the pillows can get a bit beat up, don't use your best decorative pillows. Also, the pillows need to be free of buttons, exposed zippers, or rough fabrics. These things can hurt your hands while you are punching.

Once you have your pillows, kneel or sit on the floor and pile the pillows up in front of you. The space that surrounds you needs to be clear. So position yourself several feet away from any walls, doors, furniture, or the like.

Begin increasing your breath, wiggling your hands and fingertips, moving your torso, neck, spine and head, gradually increasing your intake of oxygen. Once you have your breath going, begin focusing on whatever you're feeling angry or frustrated about. Let those feelings come to the surface. When you're fully in touch with those feelings, begin hitting the pillows in front of you. I don't mean mild actions. I mean really slamming them! Punch those pillows as hard as you can!

Use both hands in unison, or beat the pillows alternating your right and left fists. If your pillows fall to the side, stop and pile them up again. Be sure to avoid hitting the floor with your fists or any other hard surface! That'll really hurt. Continue punching until you must rest.

Then sit back, take a few breaths, feel the release and expansion inside your body. Notice how big you feel energetically. Feel the heat. Sense your inner strength and power.

Now, with your newfound sense of the enormity, go for another round. Focus on the feelings and begin pounding the pillows again. Really let yourself feel the anger.

• **Punching A Punching Bag**—Just like punching pillows, but you can do it at the gym during your workout. Nobody has to know. Just let your feelings come up and go for it! To intensify the experience, imagine those people you're angry with are the bag. Let 'em know how it feels to be put down, beat up, or abused. Let 'em have it!

• **Punching Pillows And Screaming**—This exercise is similar to the one described above, only we add our voices, just as we did when screaming in pillows.

Because nothing is covering your mouth, the sounds can be loud and disturbing to others. Therefore, before you do this exercise, be sure your environment is suitable—that you are home alone or in a space in which you will not be alarming or bothering those around you. Turn up the volume on the stereo so if others are nearby, they'll hear the music and not you.

• **Hitting A Mattress With A Bat**—Get a whiffle bat or a plain old baseball bat. Sit or kneel beside your bed or in front of a few large piled pillows. Begin to breathe, moving your body, fingertips, and arms focusing on your emotions. Then, as you did when punching pillows, let the anger or rage fill you and start hitting the mattress as hard as you can with the bat. Continue hitting vigorously, with no restraints! Let the energy move. Let yourself really feel whatever is there—the hatred, the rage, or the terror. Stop and rest when you're tired. Go for a few more rounds until you feel your release is complete. Then sense inside your body the expansion, the hugeness!

• **Beating A Mattress With Your Arms And Legs**— This exercise is great when you feel *really really* enraged, frustrated, or upset. Clear off your bed, then lie down in the middle of it. Begin breathing deeper, moving your body and fingertips. Increase your breath and focus on your authentic emotions. Then, as you feel the emotions, begin to express them by kicking your legs and pounding your fists. Really let it happen. The bed will hold you, so just let it all pour out with all the intensity you can muster. Really go for it through several rounds.

You can also use your voice with this, yelling sounds or words. Use a pillow to cover your mouth or, if the environment is suitable, yell with no pillow. When you feel like you can't possibly do one more punch or kick, close your eyes and feel what it's like inside your body. Sense your enormity. Experience the bodily-felt sense of power and might. Know this is your true nature, who you are.

Resting Afterward When you have completed any of these exercises—creative or therapeutic—always take a few moments afterwards to rest easily with your eyes closed, and sense inside your body. Breathe deeply and feel as much as you can feel, see as much as you can see, know as much as you can know.

It's not about hitting the pillows; it's about letting your anger move out through the act of hitting, and letting yourself feel the power that comes from freeing those pent-up emotions. It's about feeling what is authentic, letting it move and reconnecting with the part of yourself that has been lost: your essential self.

When you let the monster out and release your pent-up emotions, you reconnect with your inner self. Whatever essential quality you may have needed, like love or acceptance or strength, will arise naturally and fill you. Often that quality is subtle and easily overlooked. So, just be quiet for a few minutes and feel what is happening on a delicate level. Then embody those qualities as you WALK TALL through your daily life.

Follow the Thread

Here is a more gentle therapeutic method.

This technique requires staying alert and present to

whatever is happening in the moment. It requires letting go of our *preference* to experience only what is pleasant and, instead, be willing to experience whatever is there, even if it is *unpleasant*. As we go deeper, things from our past that have been undigested (where the energy has been blocked and repressed) begin to arise. We can then repair the break in the flow of energy by feeling and tolerating it.

Stay with what's juicy—follow the thread of your experience that has the most intensity and depth.

You will experience a tendency to get distracted. That means once you start to bring to consciousness emotions that have been tucked away for a long time, they will fight to remain submerged in the unconscious. They will do just about anything to pull your attention in other directions, thereby interfering with Following the Thread. So beware!

For example: you could start Following the Thread, sensing your fear about a presentation you have to give tomorrow at work. You close your eyes, take a few deep breaths, then notice some yucky sensation in your belly. As you put your attention there, you have the thought, "What are we going to do with the kids tonight?" This totally *unrelated* thought is a defense mechanism. Its purpose is to keep your awareness on the surface and not let you see what's so neatly hidden under the carpet of your unconscious. Its purpose is to maintain the "status quo" and discourage change, which includes growth. This is the "trickster"—a definite force to contend with. Sometimes the trickster will make you feel overwhelmingly sleepy, like a wet army blanket of fatigue has just been thrown on you. Naturally, you respond by thinking, "I feel so tired, I have to lie down this instant and go to sleep." This is just what the defense wants you to do: not gain awareness. Don't lie down and go to sleep. Open your eyes and look around. Move your body. Get up and walk around if you need to. Then begin again.

Another tactic of the trickster is to distract you. You might be in a deep state, or recalling an important memory, then suddenly you hear a voice out the window. All you can think about is that voice. Or you think of something you forgot to do today, and feel an urgent need to get up that moment and attend to it.

These forces tend to keep us small and weak and afraid. They discourage our growth because, somewhere deep inside, we are afraid of change. But we must be cautious and not get snared by the trickster. We must be BIG and alert and do our best to stay on track.

This is when working with an effective therapist or teacher can be imperative. These professionals stand back from your experience; they're not caught up in it. It's much easier for them to see the trickster and help you avoid getting swayed. They can help you see the "bigger picture" and view your situation from a broader perspective. They have been down this road. They know the territory and have a much better idea of what might be coming or what might be needed.

Because of their knowledge and experience, they can provide guidance for those new to this territory.

Experience also may be the distinguishing factor between a teacher/therapist who is effective and one who is not.

You'll know you are finished (for now) when your experience has transformed from unpleasant to pleasant, from constricting to expansive. Sense the expanded state as deeply as possible. Remember it. Know this is the truth. Take this experience with you into your life.

What does the Bible say? "The kingdom of God lies within." All the love, all the power, all the peace you could ever want is right there inside of you. All you need to do is uncover what's already there by transforming your emotions into essence. Doing the Monster Dance is one path. There are certainly many others. But this one works. Try it out and see for yourself.

Here are two exercises to get you warmed up for doing the Monster Dance:

EXERCISE I Hate It When...

In your journal, write "I hate it when..." on the first line. Then fill in the blank. Continue in a like manner down the page for as many pages as you want. Let your authentic feelings come up to the surface and let out your pent-up anger.

Here are some examples:
- I hate it when people stare at me.
- I hate that I can't kick them.
- I hate that my mom is dead.
- It really makes me mad that losing weight is so difficult.

- I hate it when I'm upset and no one seems to notice.
- I hate that…
- I'm enraged when…

You can vary the opening phrase, but stay with the theme of things that make you angry, resentful or enraged. Be specific. You can do this exercise as often as you wish. You might find it helpful especially after getting upset at something or someone. Remember, this list is for you, no one else.

After you write the list, you have some good material to go to the pillows with. Find one or two things on your list that upset you the most. When the time is right, pile up your pillows or get on your bed and Express and Release! Or do the Monster Dance. Let your anger have a voice and a space. Let your true emotions move!

EXERCISE I Want…

This exercise is similar to the previous one, only this time list things you desire, long for, and want. Getting in touch with what you want supports the expansion of independence and will. For example:

- I want new tires for my car.
- I want more harmony in my relationship.
- I want to know myself better.
- I really want flowers in my garden.
- I want to silence my inner critic.
- I really want…
- I want…

When this list is complete, pick one and then

practice following the thread. Start with allowing yourself to feel your longing for whatever, and see where it takes you. Afterward, write down your experience in your journal. Do this as often as you like.

PART TWO
CONCLUSION

The dynamic forms of the Monster Dance may be intimidating to you. But *anyone* can write a poem, beat a drum or draw a picture. As you transform your ugly emotions into something beautiful, something powerful, you wash the windows of perception. When you are BIG inside and allow emotions you have long ago repressed, to move—Express and Release safely—something astounding happens. What lies beneath the surface of you is revealed: essential ingredients for successful living like courage, confidence and compassion! So, stretch a little. Break out of that stiff box. Do the Monster Dance and discover within yourself everything you need to WALK TALL!

PART THREE

UNVEILING

THE DIAMOND

WITHIN

INTRO: FINDING YOUR TRUE SELF

When you do something like take a walk, express thoughts, or make something new, you do it from your sense of self. It is from this notion that you make all movements out into the world—all expressions, creations, and manifestations. It is vitally important, therefore, that your sense of self be positive, healthy, and robust!

As children, we came to know who we were and formed our sense of self from the impressions and reactions of those around us. Most of the people who saw us as young children perceived us only on a superficial level—how we looked, behaved, and performed. Not many of us were fortunate to get mirroring from parents and others who had the capacity to see through to our depths, to who we truly were. As a result, most of us saw ourselves in the light of our surface flaws.

This is a great misfortune. Yet, as adults, we can remedy the situation. We can expand beyond superficial perception and experience ourselves in a deep way, as we truly are: magnificent and whole.

This process requires valuing inner life and a deep love for the truth. Going through this process will set you free from limitations and suffering from your past. It will release you into a new life of purpose, meaning, and fulfillment.

I call it unveiling the diamond within, for it involves turning your gaze from the outside to the inside, from the superficial to the depth, from the false to the true. Unveiling the diamond is the process of recognizing the truth of who you are and allows you to move from that truth out into the world.

❶

INNER LIFE

BALANCING INNER AND OUTER LIFE

Imagine the video game PAC Man with the little yellow mouth-man that zooms around the screen. Hear his insidious squawk—waka... waka.. waka... Running around.... waka... waka... waka.... eating up dots... waka... waka... forever. Eating up everything in its path...waka...waka...waka... Endlessly, waka...waka... waka....as if nothing will ever satisfy its hunger or tame its pointless existence.

"
*Who looks
outside dreams;
who looks
inside wakes.*
"

—C.G. JUNG

PAC Man personifies my take on the soul of mainstream culture: we eat a smorgasbord of experiences but *nothing* can fill the hole. Nothing satisfies for more than a moment or so. Yet the chase for more never ends.

Most of us have been led to believe a life spent in

acquiring *outer* glories will provide us with happiness, peace, and fulfillment. Is this the case? Are people content? Are you?

How many times have we heard about the millionaire who is unhappy, unsatisfied with his or her life. Think of Marilyn Monroe—enormously successful on the outside, yet she committed suicide. Outer glories don't satisfy many of us for more than a moment or so. Not long after the win, discontent winds up, and we're off again running after our next "fix."

A German proverb says, "What is the use of running if we are not on the right road?" Perhaps the road our modern western culture is taking us down is not the right road. Perhaps the culture is missing something. Perhaps it seeks only outer gratification. Perhaps we suffer from an immense inner emptiness and sense of pointlessness.

Think about a hamster running on its hamster wheel. The little fuzzy rodent runs like mad, with all its might, faster and faster, harder and harder. But goes NO WHERE. Many people are constantly doing, constantly worrying, constantly busy. But ultimately, they may be running nowhere. In the end, and hopefully in between, they stop and ask, "What is all this busyness for? What am I doing?" Many arrive at their deathbeds only to mumble, "Is that all there is?"

When something imperative is missing, we can see it. We can see it in the daze of the elderly. We can see it in the rampant consumerism. We can see it in the annual expenditures on prescription (and nonprescription) drugs.

The problem: lack of balance between inner and outer life. How much attention does our culture place on what's happening *outside* of us, compared to what's going on *inside*? When was the last time you saw a TV commercial advertising inner peace?

The soul-ution? Spend more time, focus, energy, and money attending, developing, and honoring what is going on *inside*.

Developing an inner life is not just about getting in touch with our feelings, our intuitions, even our relationship with God. It's also about growing the ability to be content. Contentment does not equate with accomplishment or success. It means being at peace with how things *are*—successful or not so successful. It means being able to stop running; to stop eating up experiences like a PAC Man eats up the dots. Nurturing an inner life enhances our ability to enjoy—simply, thoroughly, and profoundly.

There is more. Developing an inner life goes hand in hand with developing a sense of purpose and meaning. Many people in today's world feel lost, bewildered. "What's the point of my existence? Who am I really?" they wonder.

These questions whisper inside of us all. Many people do not hear the subtle voice encouraging them to become a complete and whole human being because they are distracted by chasing and running. Quieting down allows those questions to be heard and answered. If they're not answered, can we truly be at peace?

WALKING TALL is an inner thing. It happens not because of your outer stature—physical, political, or economic—but because of your inner size. So to grow a sense of inner bigness, learn how to nurture the garden of your inner life.

NURTURE AN INNER LIFE

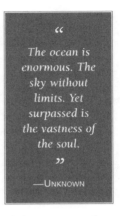

"
The ocean is enormous. The sky without limits. Yet surpassed is the vastness of the soul.
"

—UNKNOWN

Nurturing an inner life means developing a relationship with that "stuff" that goes on inside of you. This happens quite naturally when you start paying attention to your thoughts, feelings, bodily sensations, emotions, and intuitions. Inner life also consists of the deeper parts of self, such as spirit and soul, essence and Being. Nurturing an inner life means connecting with those more subtle aspects of yourself, bridging the gap between material life and spiritual life, between feeling like a separate entity and sensing a connection with all that is.

As you develop an inner life, your sense of emptiness relaxes and an inner fullness begins to unfold. This blossoming creates the foundation for peace, contentment, and real happiness.

Developing your inner life helps connect you to your purpose, to your guidance, and to all that is. It nourishes real relationships and the flow of real love. It supports ease and enjoyment of this wondrous thing called life. It opens you to deeper and richer dimensions of living, loving, sensing, and Being. It allows you to be touched deeply, to feel deeply, and to act sincerely. It supports honesty and integrity. It colors the "little things" in life with delight. It heals wounds of the past. It equips you with strength, wisdom, joy, and compassion. It enchants you with endless mystery and wonder. It helps you WALK TALL.

As one of my favorite blues singers, Keb Mo, says, "There is more than one way Home." And there is certainly more than one way to develop an inner life. The main thing is to devote a portion of your day, small or big, to focusing on what is going on *inside* of you.

Inner Guidance Like Dorothy on the road to Oz, do we take the road to the right, or the road to the left? Do we proceed quickly or slowly? Do we go alone or with others? Frequently when faced with a tough decision, people look outside themselves to obtain guidance. Experts in a field usually know more, after all. But many times we need to make a decision about our life's direction. These are the times when the only expert is ourself. No one knows us better than we do.

Everyone has an inner guide that offers free advice and direction on just about anything. This guidance comes from a broader and higher perspective—a "Big Self"—many call it the "Higher Self." It supports our evolution and growth. When you listen inside, can you hear its voice? Or have you lost connection with your inner guide?

For a long time, I didn't hear my inner voice. But as I did many of the practices described in this chapter, especially the Kath meditation, I gradually developed the capacity to hear that quiet, subtle, yet ever-so-wise voice from within.

Several years ago, I was fortunate to have the opportunity to buy a home. My financial advisor referred me to a lovely realtor in town. I called Kate that afternoon and made an appointment. We sat down and I told her as clearly as I could what I wanted in my new home, what I didn't want, how much I could afford, and what kind of neighborhood I wanted to be in. I was single at the time, so I was tackling this mission solo.

I was so excited the following day as we ventured out on our first day of "house shopping." We drove from one end of town to the other, going into several beautiful homes—upstairs, downstairs, front yards, back yards. All had potential, but none felt quite right. I met with the realtor every day that week and hunted high and low, but still no hits. That weekend, I went home with a stack of "drive-bys" to check. I went downtown, out into the country...I drove by at least 25 homes.

The following week, we sniffed through the ones that showed some potential. Everything a "near miss." This went on for several weeks. In about the sixth week, Kate, now my good friend, began to get antsy. That Friday afternoon, she tried talking me into settling for a red brick house that wasn't quite right. But I didn't go along with her coaxing.

Then Saturday morning, I woke up feeling particularity energized and clear. Lying in bed, I thought, "I'm going to get in my car and just drive around. I'm going to let my inner guide direct me." I threw on some clothes, hopped in my car, and headed toward a neighborhood on the edge of town where the lots were big. Kate and I hadn't looked there because, as I later found out, it was in the "flood zone."

As I approached the neighborhood, I drove slowly and began tuning in to my whispering guide. The streets in that neighborhood were quite twisty, so after going just a few blocks, I got totally lost. Which way now? I wondered. I took a right here, then straight, then a few lefts. Then I found myself on a street I had never been on before, a dead-end street. My radar immediately spotted a "For Sale" sign on the front lawn of one of the houses. The hair on the back of my neck stood up and I zipped in front of the house. I glanced up. My jaw dropped. It was perfect!

I scanned the written territory seeking my prey: the phone number. As I read it more carefully, I noticed it said "For Sale by Owner." No wonder we hadn't seen this house listed in the MLS, I thought. Faster than a speeding bullet, I dialed that number on my cell phone. The owner said to come back in an hour.

That hour seemed like weeks. When the time came, I knocked on the front door and stepped inside the house. Within the first 30 seconds, I said, "This is it! I'll take it!"

This house had everything I had been looking for—no compromises. The windows were low enough, I could see out of them in every room. The rooms had a lot of light and a spacious feel. Located on a quiet street away from any buzzing main streets, its lot was twice the size of most. And the house was only seven years old. It had air conditioning, windows that opened and closed easily, and light switches I could reach easily. It was not in the flood zone. Best of all, it was within my price range.

As I shook the seller's hand on my way out, I sighed a deep breath of relief. I had found my perfect home...**my inner guide** had led me there.

Inner guidance is also important because life has no universal rules: that is, no laws that apply to each and every situation. Take the rule about telling a lie. Telling a lie is *wrong*. But let's imagine you are living in Nazi

Germany, hiding a Jewish family in your home. You hear a knock at the door. A Gestapo officer asks if any Jews are in your home. This is a time when breaking the rule about lying would be the *right* thing to do. No rule holds true in every situation. So, although we can rely on rules for some direction, we also need guidance of a higher and more personal source.

Our inner guide is perhaps the best friend we will ever have. It is the light that directs us through the dark mysteries of this life. So tune in. Listen to what that friendly voice inside is saying. Trust it. Respect it!

INQUIRE

Inquiry is the process of investigating what is true. To build your inner life, inquire into the truth of your experience in the present moment. If you stay with what is happening now, what unfolds next? If you stay present with that, where does it take you?

You can inquire into a variety of things, like a motivation or a hunch. What did I just feel? What made me react this way? Why did I choose this relationship? Why do I keep losing track of time? We can inquire into any of our experiences.

> "
> *It is the personal, free, alone investigation of your moment to moment truth, that will lead you to the truth, all levels of the truth.*
> "
> —A.H. ALMAAS

Inquiry takes you from the surface of what is happening to a deeper level of experience and understanding. Many times, it uncovers what has been hidden in the unconscious mind, like peeling an onion. One layer is revealed, then the next, then the next. As you descend inwardly, you come closer to the truth of not only what is taking place but, ultimately and eventually, to the truth of your Self.

Long before the idea or language of WALKING TALL was born, terms referring to differing parts of our internal self existed: the "Big Self" and the "little self." The Big Self is universal, unbounded, and connected to all that is. The Big Self is said to be the "true" self, the more substantial and unchanging aspect of self.

The little self refers to the part on the surface—one's personality and individuality. It is said to be the "false" self, the part that is changing, evolving, and growing. Big Self is an expresssion of your Being; little self is an expression of your ego.

The process of inquiry takes you from the surface of the little self to the depth of the Big Self. As you inquire into the experiences of the little self, more and more will be revealed about both the Big and little self—about what's true and false.

What is true right now? This is the theme of inquiry. It guides you to deeper and deeper levels of the truth. So, inquire into the nature of your experience at any given moment and see where it leads you.

Here is where inquiry led me as I Followed the Thread:

I stood in the background listening to the soft music, my heart aching. "Why? Why am I feeling so sad right now?"

Coming into the final hours of my Group Leadership Training, we were transitioning into a group exercise. The women were told to choose a male partner for a slow dance.

As the sauntering melody filled the room, I felt nauseous and shrank into the shadows in the back of the room. From there I watched the men holding the women closely to their chests. I noticed a fragrance of romance in the air. I wanted to disappear and die. But why?

I remembered that, ever since junior high school, slow music always made me feel sick to my stomach. What was as I supposed to do? Go out there and stick my face in the crotch of my latest crush as we snuggled up? Or should I stand on a chair or a table and make a total spectacle of myself, and him?

As the music continued to sway, I felt my chest fill with a sorrow as heavy as brown dirt. My breath constricted. My mind flooded with memories of all the average-sized people I had wanted to embrace—and be embraced by in return—but didn't because of my short stature.

I looked over at my friend and ally, Mukara. She reached out, inviting me to dance. I hesitantly stepped out from the darkness. Mukara stood less than five feet tall, so my head rested on her chest.

She lovingly embraced me. I could sense her acceptance of me as I was. I stayed with the feelings and continued to inquire.

The feelings I had been holding back now took one more step toward the surface. Acknowledging what was there, I allowed the tears to come forth. I began weeping with no restraints, like a young child.

Mukara felt me shaking. She looked with eyes of compassion into mine. With her support, I let myself digest this old pain that I had been holding at bay for a long, long time. As I did, the pain began to evaporate.

"What?" Mukara asked, directing my inquiry further. I tried to catch my breath. Then I whispered the words scraping across my heart, "I just want to be the same size."

As these words took shape, I realized they had been there every time I stood in the background watching my friends dance. That same longing resurfaced. But this time I let myself really feel it.

Mukara's smile glowed with tenderness. She responded, "And you're not the same size. You are three and a half feet tall and will remain three and a half feet tall."

She spoke then to the part of me that needs to know what is possible and what is not. She spoke to a long-ago wish that my destiny of living this life as a little person might change. She spoke to the part of me that needed to accept reality as it is. Given the depth of her presence and her total acceptance, her words did not hurt me. Rather, they gave me a firm ground to stand on.

Something then shifted throughout my entire body. Something released. I noticed the music had changed—much faster now. Mukara and I both took a step back and started to boogie. What's happening inside of me now? I sensed my body. It felt like a cool pool—each movement of my hips was like a rippling wave across the water. Then I felt a huge space in my heart and a soft yellow glow: the presence of joy. The music penetrated all the way down to my bones. I moved ecstatically.

With this freedom came an understanding: I was free—free from needing something outside to let me know I was lovable. In this refreshing clarity, I knew I was connected to all those lovely people without needing to touch or be touched. My heart smiled.

I felt grateful. As I continued dancing, I sensed inside and saw a large, full pink rose in the center of my chest. It sang a song, chanting, "I am love." The remembrance of who I truly was. You see, the truth had set me free.

SLOW DOWN

These four practices can help you slow down, turn your attention inward, and nurture your inner life: Stopping, Sensing Yourself, Yoga, and Spending Time Alone.

Stopping

"Stopping" is a very simple and brilliant way to create balance between your inner and outer life. Invented by Dr. David Kundtz, it is described at length in his book *Stopping: How to Be Still When You Have to Keep Going.* Here's how he explains the process:

> Stopping is doing nothing, as much as possible, for a definite period of time—whether a moment or a month—for the purpose of waking up and remembering who you are.
>
> So, most importantly, Stopping is doing nothing, spending time with nothing specifically to do. It can be from a few seconds to a few hours (These are Stillpoints). It can be a whole day or a weekend (Stopovers). It can even be a longer time, a few weeks or a month or more (Grinding Halts).
>
> And what do you "do" during these times? Again, nothing. And just how do you do nothing? Just hang out, breathe, walk, sit, mess around, pace, gaze out the window, wander down the lane, observe, notice, daydream, take a break, slowly drink a glass of water, be still,

practice smiling, stretch. The list is limitless—it is limited only by your lack of comfort with what you might call "down time."

We are such a rushed society, zooming through life as if running scared. We tend to treat moments of stillness as strangers, even as enemies, or at best as a waste of time.

I guarantee that a day punctuated with little moments-of-doing-nothing will bring you to its end more refreshed and centered than you might expect. And a whole afternoon of doing nothing could become the cornerstone of your week.

Stopping will keep your life your life, since it is based on the belief that it is vitally important to know what and whom you deeply care about, and, as Friedrich Von Hugel said decades ago, "Caring is the greatest thing, caring matters most."

The best things about Stopping are:

- It is totally simple, you probably already do it in some way (now make it intentional).
- It is easy (you just do nothing in whatever you can at the moment).
- And it's enjoyable (this is time of rest, renewal, with no agenda).

Notice, notice, notice! Then—slowly—life begins to make more sense.

EXERCISE Stillpoint

(from *Stopping* by David Kundtz)

A *Stillpoint* is one of the most simple and quick stopping moments.

Pause a moment and stay as you are, reading this book.

- Now, briefly relax your body as much as possible, letting go of tensions.
- Then take a deep, relaxing breath. S-l-o-w-l-y take another.
- Now think of someone, or something, you love or enjoy. Got it in mind?
- Okay. Softly close your eyes for five or ten seconds as you gently hold that image of what you love in your mind.

That's it! That's stopping. This is just one example of a Stillpoint; others include a Pause, a Breath, a Remembering. You can take a Stillpoint anytime, anywhere.

When you come to the end of a day with many Stillpoints, you'll feel more relaxed, more awake and—most importantly—more ready to go on.

Sensing Yourself

Sensing yourself is as simple as putting your attention on your arms and legs. The purpose is to bring your whole self—mind, body, and spirit—into your present experience. It strengthens your capacity to take in the richness of each moment through all your senses. It supports objective perception. It intensifies your sense of presence and develops the capacity to experience contentment.

Sensing yourself can be done at any time, during any activity. You can do it while brushing your teeth, walking your dog, talking on the phone, running a mile, or lying in bed.

You can do it right now. As you continue reading, turn part of your awareness to your body. What position are your arms in right now? Are they tired from holding this book, or relaxed on the arm of your chair? What about your legs? Where are they right now? How do they feel? Cramped, stressed, relaxed?

This is sensing yourself. Notice any differences? Has your vision or hearing heightened? Are you more aware of your surroundings? Are you more conscious of your body? Probably.

It's easy to sense your arms and legs while you are doing a basic chore like typing, hanging laundry, or washing dishes. If you continue sensing your arms and legs every time you do that same chore, after a while remembering will become automatic. As you do the task, you'll naturally begin sensing your limbs.

Eating is another good time to practice sensing your self. Pay attention to your body. Slow down and focus on what you are *tasting*. See how much more flavor the food has? Sense your abdomen. Are you really hungry? Do you need to eat, or are you just tempted because the food looks or smells good? Are you comfortably full yet? Is it time to stop eating? Sensing yourself before eating and during meals is a great way to keep your natural figure, or shrink into it.

Practice sensing your self as often as you can.

Yoga

Yoga engages the entire body in bending, stretching, and breathing. It relieves tension and stress and helps you slow down. It increases your body's strength and flexibility, brings you into the present moment, and opens the door to your inner dimensions. It nurtures your inner life. The benefits of Yoga encompass the whole person—mind, body and spirit—as expressed in these quotes:

> Hospitals throughout the country are using yoga and meditation to help patients suffering from chronic pain and stress-related medical disorders.
>
> Yoga is not a religion. It is a nonsectarian method for promoting a healthy and harmonious lifestyle. Any person of any faith can practice yoga and find his or her religion enhanced as a result.
>
> –Suza Francina,
> *The New Yoga for People Over 50*

> Yoga differs from other types of rehabilitative exercise in that it engages the whole person. Yoga-based relaxation techniques and strengthening exercises are effective because the mind is focused in a meditative way on your movements, skin and muscle sensations, and relaxed breathing. Mind and body work together, creating a physiological and psychological

environment that optimizes the potential for healing.

−Mary Pullig Schatz, M.D.,
Back Care Basics

Health is reflected in lifestyle, and if we ignore our bodies we may, even by our mid-thirties, stiffen far more than necessary. Movement lubricates the muscles, ligaments, and joints. ...Stretching daily can reduce the stiffness, allowing us eventually to dance, play tennis, and enjoy our bodies well into our real old age.

−Maxine Tobias,
Complete Stretching

The best way to learn Yoga is from a teacher. You can understand the postures and the breath that goes with them while listening to and looking at an instructor. A teacher can also correct mistakes and help you "get it right" before you develop bad habits.

Yoga has gained much popularity over the last several years. Classes are offered at most local Y's, health clubs, and fitness centers. Learning Yoga postures from a book is also an option. But if possible, take a few classes, then refer to your books for further guidance.

Several types of Yoga offer a range of challenge and intensity. My experience with Yoga is somewhat limited but I'd like to share it.

My favorite type of Yoga is Bikram's, which is done in a room about 95 to 100 degrees Fahrenheit. The heat has two benefits: 1) It makes you sweat, which purifies the body of toxins. 2) It warms your muscles, which gives them their maximum stretching ability.

In Bikram's, the Yoga teacher describes how to do each posture as you go in and out of it. The series of postures is the same every time. Once you learn the routine, you can focus more of your attention on what's going on inside. This type of Yoga offers both a challenging and a hearty workout. To find a Bikram's studio in your area, look in the phonebook under "Yoga University."

Asthanga is another form of Yoga I'm familiar with. I suggest it for those who enjoy lots of movement. Asthanga, like a flowing dance, involves continuous, fluid movements between each posture. Asthanga can be tough but adds vitality and strength to the body, clarity to the mind, and peace to the spirit.

Hatha Yoga is perhaps the most common and well-known Yoga practiced in the U.S. Along with Iyengar Yoga, both are gentle and relaxing, yet rejuvenating and dynamic at the same time.

All types of Yoga are taught at varying levels, beginner, intermediate, and advanced. Try out different types of Yoga and find what works best for you. You'll know because you enjoy the practice and feel rejuvenated, alert, and joyful afterward.

Spending Time Alone

If we don't learn to spend time alone, we are bound to a need—a need to be with others. Dependency is like a weighty chain we carry around with us. Others feel the burden of it, as well.

For some people, spending time alone can be scary because it may be unfamiliar, or because it leaves them without a sense of external connection or protection. For people who have filled their lives with social interaction, learning how to spend time alone might be a challenging endeavor.

"
The worst loneliness is not being comfortable with yourself.

"

—MARK TWAIN

Think of your hours spent alone as an ally. Alone time allows you to reflect, relax, and rejuvenate. It gives you a chance to dream, scheme, and envision your future. It supports you in getting to know yourself, what's going on inside, what works in your life and what doesn't. It lets you get in touch with how you feel and what you really think. Time alone helps build independence, leadership, and courage. It adds a dimension to your life that may not otherwise be there: depth.

Spending time alone does not mean you have to sit in a corner and stare into space. There are lots of things to do. Journal writing is one of my favorites and offers many benefits. By writing about your thoughts and feelings, you get to know yourself in a different way than ever before. Insights often arise, as well as an awareness of your critical voice. Journaling provides the privacy to express your disappointments, your dreams, even your resentments. You can congratulate yourself for your successes. You can reflect on a past event. You can give yourself a pep talk after a failure. You can contemplate the lessons your challenges may be bringing you, and list the areas of growth you notice within yourself.

Spend time alone in nature. Find a place that feels like a sanctuary to you, some comforting, quiet, and beautiful spot. Seek out several environments like this and visit them often. See how your spirit is renewed. Walk, sit, smell, swim, jog, meditate, contemplate, paint, write, pray. Listen to the silence. Look closely at the beauty that surrounds you. Notice the smile on your face and the peace inside your body. Let these things nourish you.

Other fun activities to do by yourself: hiking, biking, creating art, exercising, or cleaning out your closet. You can take a quiet approach and pray, meditate, contemplate, or sense yourself. You can work on setting goals, evaluating your progress, acknowledging your wins. You can cook, eat, read, or watch a movie. And you can always count all your blessings!

Once you make friends with yourself, it's easier to make outside friends, and keep them. So walk in the woods, sit on a mountaintop, write a poem. All of these things increase your capacity to have a life enriched from the inside out.

MEDITATE

Meditation offers a marvelous opportunity to turn your attention inward. It is simple to do and allows the body to have a deep state of rest, providing significant rejuvenation. Meditation releases deep stress and provides a gateway into the depth of inner life. Meditation fertilizes inner life and inner bigness.

Some meditations are done sitting, walking, or doing simple tasks. Some with eyes closed, some with eyes open. Some with a mantra to help focus attention inward, others by following the breath. Some are learned from a personal teacher and others from a book. Whichever way you choose, I suggest trying a few variations until you find one that works best for you.

> "
> *Transcendental Meditation opens the awareness to the infinite reservoir of energy, creativity and intelligence that lies within everyone.*
> "
>
> —MAHARISHI MAHESH YOGI

My "career" of higher learning began the fall after my high school graduation. At the ripe age of 18, I left home and headed for The University of Hartford in Connecticut.

One October day, I was on my way out of the Literature building. I stopped in front of the bulletin board, suddenly taken by a photo of a man in a white robe with long hair. He appeared to be from India and the poster indicated there would be a talk in a few days. I read these words on the poster below his photo: "The nature of life is bliss!" I smiled. Wouldn't that be nice? I pondered.

Fumbling through my backpack, I found a pen to write down the details of the advertised event. When the evening finally arrived, I eagerly made my way to the hall in anxious anticipation of meeting an Indian guru. To my dismay, no guru showed up, not even an Indian man. Only an American gentleman dressed in a suit and tie. This was the early '70s; nobody wore a suit and a tie on a college campus!

Hmm, I thought as I crossed my arms and slouched down in my chair. As he spoke, that age-old adage came to mind: don't judge a book by its cover. I relaxed after a while and noticed my head nodding a confirming "yes" to all he said. It sounded good, wholesome, true.

A few weeks later, I arrived at the meditation center and met my teacher, Bob. We went into a small room and he taught me the Transcendental Meditation (TM) technique in just a few moments. As soon as I closed my eyes and started meditating, my body began to melt like butter in the sun. All the tension let go as I soaked up a deep state of silence and profound relaxation. How pleasant, how peaceful, I thought. More than that, I felt like I had come Home.

During that first year of regular meditation, I enjoyed many benefits from my daily practice: increased mental alertness, improved concentration, and better memory. Good gear to include in the toolbox of an aspiring college freshman.

I befriended several "meditators" that year.

They became like a warm fire on cold stormy nights. You see, this campus was perhaps the snobbiest and most highly prejudiced place I had ever been. My roommate did not speak one word to me for the entire three months we shared a room. I guess conversing with a Little Person was too far beneath her soaring social status. When I joined folks to eat in the cafeteria, they'd frequently get up and move to another table. People stared at me so much, I felt like an animal in a zoo. This was among the most difficult years of my life. My meditation and meditation friends, however, offered welcome solace.

At the end of the year, my closest girlfriend, Corrine, told me about a university in Iowa associated with TM. Without "meditating" much about it at all, I transferred to Maharishi International University.

The following college years were happy, even ecstatic. Everyone at the university honored inner life. Everyone there meditated twice a day. Everyone there was well rested, joyful, and awake. And we got high, oh yes, high, on meditation. Something about the sober aliveness, about the purity of hearts, about the daily plunge to our inner depths, gave rise to relationships of a different quality than any I had ever known or

top:
A Hawaiian Luau

right bottom:
Toga! Toga! My 24th
surprise birthday party

have known since. These relationships were blessed; they glistened with what was real.

A sense of unity prevailed through my years living in this heavenly community. During this era, my inner life was born and well nurtured; my heart was full of joy and my life was filled with love. I can't say enough wonderful things about this particular form of meditation. It definitely worked, and still works, for me now after almost thirty years.

After leaving the TM community in Iowa, I was

introduced to many other forms of meditation, which I found valuable as well. All of them helped me be more of who I was, not who others said I had to be. All of them helped me expand my notions about what was possible. All of them helped me experience more depth and richness in my every moment. All of them helped me accept what is as it is, and most importantly, accept myself. All of them helped me *be* much more than I ever thought possible. *(For more information on Transcendental Meditation, please refer to the Resource List.)*

If you'd like to start meditating immediately, these three forms of meditation can help direct your attention inward and expand your inner dimensions.

• **Follow Your Breath** If you haven't practiced meditation before, now is a good time to start. Sit in a comfortable chair with a back support. Close your eyes. Begin by putting your attention on your breath as it moves in and out of your lungs. Gradually, let your breathing deepen, taking bigger and bigger inhalations. Then balance the inhalation and exhalation so each one takes the same amount of time. Continue to place simple awareness on your breath as it moves in and out.

You might notice that it's easy to get distracted by noises. You might hear voices or cars. You might also get distracted by your thoughts. During meditation, it's common to have all sorts of thoughts about all sorts of things relating to the past, the future, or today. When you notice you have been distracted, gently bring your attention back to your breath as it moves in and out. Sit there quietly and continue meditating for 10 to 15 minutes.

When you finish, open your eyes and look around the room. Slowly stretch. Give yourself a few minutes to "come back" to the space. Then gently transition into your next activity. If you feel lightheaded, sit down and stretch for another minute or two.

• **Kath Meditation** The Kath is a point located in your body's center. This meditation brings your awareness to that place and facilitates opening the "feeling center" in your belly. It also helps gain access to your inner guidance.

Place your hand on your abdomen. Find your navel, then locate the area about an inch below your navel and about a half inch inside. That is the point of the Kath.

Once you have located your Kath, you can begin to practice the meditation. Sit comfortably in a chair or on a pillow. Close your eyes. Place your hand on your belly if it's not already there. Press in slightly with your finger at the point of your Kath to help keep your awareness there. Sense that area as you slowly breathe in and out. With your next inhalation, imagine your Kath is a point of bright white light.

As oxygen begins to fill your stomach and chest area, visualize the white light softening to yellow light as it expands into a huge sun or yellow balloon. As you exhale, see the light get smaller and more condensed, gradually shifting from yellow to white. When all the air is out, visualize a white shining star at the point of your Kath. Continue breathing in this fashion; see the light grow—getting bigger, softer, and more yellow as your belly fills up with air, then condensing and getting smaller and brighter with each exhalation. Take your hand away, relax, and continue meditating in this way for 15 minutes.

If you get distracted by thoughts or noises, gently bring your awareness back to your Kath and continue breathing and visualizing. You can do this practice once or twice a day for 15 to 20 minutes.

• **Circular Meditation** This meditation also begins at your Kath. In this practice, however, your awareness will circle your torso with each inhalation and exhalation.

To begin, sit comfortably with closed eyes. Place your awareness on your Kath and begin to take a slow, large inhalation. As you draw in air, visualize a point of light moving downward from your Kath to your lower belly and into your pelvic region, to base of your spine. Continue breathing in and allow the light to travel around to your back and up your spine, over the top of your head.

When you have taken in as much air as possible, the point of light will rest on the brow between your eyes. When you exhale, the point of light will move down the front of your body, over your chest and belly, then rest at your Kath. As you breathe in again, visualize the point of light moving down into your pelvis and then up your spine to your forehead. Exhale and let the point of light drop down to your belly center.

Repeat this as you continue to breathe in and out. If you get distracted, gently bring your awareness back to your Kath and continue with the circular breathing. You can practice for 10 to 15 minutes a day. Take a few moments to transition slowly into your other activities. Enjoy getting to know what is inside of you.

THE TRUTH WILL
SET YOU FREE

UNCOVER YOUR DEEPER SELF

After completing all my higher education—my college affiliated with meditation, Anna's dance training and photography school —I moved to Kona, Hawaii. I lived on a beautiful fruit and flower farm with several artist pals from my

> "
> *The issue is not enlightenment. The issue is not freedom. The issue is 'What is.'*
> "
>
> —A.H. ALMAAS

meditation college. We all had creative work, but spent most of our time doing our favorite job— toughing it out at the beach.

Everything on the outside was paradise. But on the **inside**—that was another story. Inside, my heart feared that I'd never find a life partner. Now,

almost 35 years old, I had not yet had a long-term love relationship.

As you've probably surmised by now, my history in intimate relationships was dreadful. Starting way back in my teen years, I wrestled with unrequited love and my longing to feel deeply accepted.

I enjoyed many lovely friendships with average-sized men in my everyday world. But they wanted nothing more than to be "just friends." The gentlemen my own size that I met at Little People conventions always lived far away. Over time, the distance wore on our ability to stay connected.

As my years as a Hawaiian "wahinee" progressed, my lack of success in the romantic arena cast a dark shadow over my idyllic surroundings. Coming up to my 40th year, my terror of spending life alone became increasingly more real. The fear got bigger and bigger, overshadowing all the benefits I had received from both my meditation and Anna's training. With each failed relationship, I gathered more and more evidence that I was, in fact, unlovable. My inner smallness blew up like a blimp. I may have delighted in swimming in the sparkling aqua waters of Kua Bay, but I was drowning in a sea of self-hatred.

Like bees around a hive, my mind swarmed with ideas about how to end the misery. I could tolerate the anguish no more. I wanted out. Driving my jeep on mountain roads, swimming in the ocean, hiking on cliffs, I continually held myself back from taking that lethal suicide step. One saving grace perhaps was my strong sense that any escape from the pain would only be temporary. What might come after death might be worse.

I awoke one morning and had a chat with God. I told God how miserable it was living with so much pain, and that I didn't want to do it anymore. I asked God to end my life or to guide me out of this hellhole.

Three weeks later, a friend arrived at the farm and told me about a unique study group called the Ridhwan School. We read together parts of a book by the founder of the school. I was intrigued by his clear expression of how we can heal deep issues, so I attended a weekend workshop to get a taste of the work.

On Saturday afternoon, our class had an opportunity to do an inquiry with the help of the teacher, Morton. While one of my classmates worked with the teacher, the rest of us listened. I got extremely upset by what one of my classmates was saying and feeling. I obviously had stuff to work on, so when she finished I raised my hand, volunteering to work with Morton next.

I don't remember the exact issue I was working with. I don't remember what happened at the beginning. But I do remember what happened toward the end of my first inquiry.

Morton asked me what I saw in my chest. I said, "A big silver metal shield. It covers my whole chest." "Can you go behind it?" he challenged. "Sure," I said confidently. Then I was silent. Morton asked what I was experiencing. "When I go behind the metal shield, there is black space, like the night sky, only there are no stars. It's totally black and completely without boundaries. It's infinite and stunningly beautiful!"

As I felt the limitless black space in each cell of my body, I heard Morton's voice, **"That is who you are,"** he stated frankly. His words sunk into me like a rock dropped in water. I didn't know how it could be, but everything in me knew he was right. "This is the truth of who you are," he reiterated. I let out a breath of relief like never before.

Sunday, I was instructed to do a "walking meditation," taking 20 minutes to walk about 25 feet and focusing on being as present as possible. I inched my knee up ever so slowly and felt the muscles pull it forward. Then, ever so gradually, I shifted my weight onto the foot that had been set down, in super slow motion. Things got very quiet inside. I continued. Then I heard a clear voice. It was my inner voice: "Your purpose is to **be here now.**" Everything inside me knew that was right.

That weekend gave me several profound insights. Afterward, I decided this program could help me break whatever cemented me together with anguish. I was astounded, yet happy, that my prayer had been answered.

I decide to commit to this path of work, also referred to as the Diamond Approach. The program uses elements from Depth Psychology combined with various spiritual practices to teach a new method of spiritual transformation in everyday life. I left Hawaii and all its splendor so I could break free from the clench of my inner smallness. I moved to Boulder, Colorado, one of two centers for the Ridhwan School, and began my serious personal work.

I had a lot of difficult times those first few years

in Boulder. Without a doubt, I had entered into the "dark night of the soul." I was at the point on the mountain climb when the air goes thin. Each step was grueling. I rarely made it through a day without crying. But every time I went into "the pit," I came out the other side with more understanding and experience of my true nature, my BIG Self.

Then I had a serendipitous experience that changed my life. I was in the thick of a six-month intensive, focusing on issues from childhood. One night, I was processing my anger about not being valued as a whole human being. I was doing a therapeutic form of the Monster Dance—beating pillows with a bat and yelling, "I hate you!" (You know, just a normal Friday night.) Because it was quite aerobic, I grew tired and lay back on my pillows to rest.

Closing my eyes, I breathed deeply to catch my breath. With each breath, I seemed to drop deeper and deeper inside myself, as if some part of me had no limits, no boundaries, no bottom.

As I lay there, still and silent, my inner vision beheld a magnificence unlike anything I'd ever experienced before. I saw a diamond! This was no "diamond in the rough!" This diamond was sheer refined **perfection!** Beyond Tiffany's, beyond royalty! Bigger than my entire body! Filling me from the top of my head to the tips of my toes. Shimmering prisms of light streamed from its center. Every facet glistened in rainbow colors. I was bathed in brilliance and beauty.

Words resounded inside of me. "**I am value. I am precious.**" I was reminded again of the truth, the truth of who I am!

In that moment, the cloak of shame and inadequacy fell to the floor. I was no longer defined by the opinion of others. I was now the authority on my worth, full to the brim with dignity.

Driving home that night, I thought if only I could be big enough to show this part of myself to others. If only I could allow myself to be precious, beautiful, and brilliant. If only I could let others see who I really am!

And that became the challenge: to avoid reverting to that small "little" person inside every time I would face difficulty, failure, or prejudice. The challenge was—and still is—to remember in every moment, in this moment, that I am that enormous shimmering diamond, that greatness which is unspeakable!

Unveiling my diamond within healed my heart, healed my life. I grew beyond knowing myself from the viewpoint of others. The perception of my intrinsic worth expanded far beyond *my superficial self. Perhaps flawed on the surface, but deep down, I came to know myself as splendidly beautiful, and as valuable as a huge shimmering diamond.*

All people have a diamond inside, just by virtue of being humans. Everyone's Being is an unfathomable mystery of wonder and beauty. We just need to turn our gaze inward and see what is there. We need to honor that Being, and inquire into whatever blocks us from experiencing it clearly, intimately.

If you miss these experiences at the beginning, don't be discouraged. I make it sound simple here, but I spent a lot of time working my way up to these revelations. I had been actively involved in my personal and spiritual growth for a few decades at that point. A lot of groundwork had been done and I had big-time support from my teachers in the Ridhwan School.

Unveiling the diamond within is only one experience of many that revealed my "true nature," my Big Self. One time, I experienced my True Self as a huge diamond, the next as unbounded black space. The next time, it arose as a pink comforting blanket, another time an ocean of love. After that came bliss, strength, power, and compassion. Then, the experience of "I Am."

Essence is Being. Being has as many different flavors, textures, and capacities as a rainbow has colors. When we stay with our experience in the moment and go deeper, whatever we need will arise. In the story above, I felt devalued. So what arose inside? My own essential value. When I feel abandoned, what arises is love. Going into hurt, compassion manifests and washes the hurt away. When feeling helpless, my own intrinsic power always comes to the rescue.

How do you unveil the diamond within and connect with your essence? Excellent question! Every page in this book contains information that will assist you in that process—making healthy choices, doing the Monster Dance, nurturing an inner life, slowing down, sensing your self, inquiring, and meditating. All these things can take you there. Only you have to be keen to *see* the diamond and then to BE it. And be willing to let go of what is false.

(For more info on the Ridhwan School, refer to Suggested Resource List.)

LET GO OF WHAT'S FALSE

People function in the world according to their identities—who they take themselves to be. For many of us, identity has to do with our names, jobs, families, social status, and so on. This is our superficial identity, or our false identity, coming from the little self.

"
We don't see things as they are, we see them as we are.
"
—THE TALMUD

Our surface identity is made of ideas, beliefs, and notions about who we are. These help us remember where we live, what we do, and how we function. They form a structure inside our mind, like an erector set. They come from our past experiences and how people responded to us, especially during early childhood. But these old ideas are most often outdated. Many of them do not serve us; often they work against us in our present adult life.

Let's take a look at the experiences of one of my psychotherapy clients to help clarify this issue.

Jamey was a 30-year-old woman who frequently complained of high anxiety when left alone for more than a few hours. Working together, we inquired into her irrational responses around being alone.

As she talked about her last episode of anxiety, I asked her to describe what was happening in her body. Jamey said, "I feel butterflies in my stomach." While focusing on that sensation for a while, she had a memory. She explained that when she was a child, she was frequently left home alone, and during that time she always felt scared.

I asked her how old she was when she was left home alone. "From age 5 to age 8 or 9," she said. "How well did you know how to take care of yourself back then?" I questioned. "Not very," she replied. "So your fear in the past made sense," I said. "How well do you know how to take care of your self now, Jamey?" "Pretty well," she confirmed.

"So, you see," I replied, "now when you are alone it reminds you of when you were left alone as a child. But the truth is you are now an adult and know how to take care of yourself. Some part of you still believes you don't know how to take care of yourself when you are alone. You must let go of the child's response to being left alone and identify with the part of you that is grown up." "I get it," she said.

The next week Jamey reported she had been "put to the test." She spent time alone on Thursday evening. "The anxiety started to mount an usual," she stated. "But then I recognized the fear was irrational, coming from my past and not the present." She further recognized that she—in the moment— was an adult who knew how to take care of herself and there was no impending threat to her safety. So she relaxed on the couch and enjoyed reading her book.

We can see clearly in this example how outdated identities can be a barrier to enjoying life. By entering into the fear and exposing the memory, Jamey located her false identity, then chose to let go of it.

It's not easy. Frequently it takes many efforts to "disidentify" from an outdated sense of self until we become liberated from it.

Take my budding career as a motivational speaker

and author as an example:

> My college buddy, Marci, had been speaking professionally for many years. In a phone conversation one day, I told her I was giving a workshop to build my psychotherapy practice. She said, "Peggy, your destiny is to be a professional speaker. Why not come with me next week to the National Speakers Association convention and learn all about the speaking business?"
>
> I went to the convention and watched the speakers "do their thing." One night at dinner, as we discussed our favorite speakers of the day, I offhandedly commented, "It looks pretty easy. Heck, I bet I could do that," and thus began my most recent career. Little did I know what I was getting myself into.
>
> As I returned to my home office the following week, I began scheming about what I might say up there on the platform. I was quite unaware of the luggage dragging behind me. In it were the following memories with countless others of a similar nature:
>
> One beautiful spring day I was walking home from grade school. I had my jacket wrapped around my waist and enjoyed the fragrance of lilacs in the air. All of a sudden, out of the corner of my eye, came disaster—a yellow school bus!

You see, we rode to school on city buses and I knew those kids on that bus didn't go to my school. They didn't know me. As the bus approached, coming closer and closer, my muscles started to freeze. I braced myself because I knew what was coming. As the bus pulled up next to me, those kids jumped out of their seats, ran over to the window, pointed their fingers at me, and nastily howled, "midget, midget, midget!" I turned my back wishing I could disappear.

Another:

During high school, I spent my summers at skating camp. However, the rink was in the middle of a snooty resort hotel. Throughout the day, I had to traverse several times between my dormitory and the skating rink. The nearly one-mile trek crossed through several patios and walkways of the hotel.

I said "snooty" because the hotel's guests were not very kind to me. They gawked and stared at me with such blatant disregard that my best friend Allison, a 5'8" slender natural-born actress, had to teach them a lesson. She would imitate their expressions in an exaggerated way as we strolled through the resort terraces.

Allison would drop her jaw as far as possible and furrow her brow to the max. She'd circle around me frantically moving your head up and down as she scanned my body. She'd point, then pretend to nudge a person next to her and chuckle.

Her overly dramatic mime was, of course, humorous to us. My pal Al also made me laugh hysterically. Laughter was a good medicine for a difficult situation. But it didn't totally soothe that reoccurring poke into my sense of value down deep in my heart.

Getting up in front of people always brings up the fear of repeating these types of experiences. When the fear comes up, I automatically identify with the child inside who was hurt so frequently, laughed at, and called names. Each time I get up to speak, I have to disidentify from those past hurtful memories and recall the truth.

It's not just with speaking in front of groups; it's also with every step of expansion I take in putting myself out there. Doing a radio interview...having my picture in the paper...being interviewed for a feature article...having articles published...publishing books...appearing on TV talk shows...doing book tours and signings. Each step of expansion brings up those old memories of being judged and ridiculed. Each time, I have to remember the truth of who I am now. I have to turn my gaze inward and sense the part of me that is huge, beautiful, precious, and wonderful-despite what others may think.

My livelihood pushes my buttons. Not that I planned it this way, but my whole life is now a part of my personal process and supports my higher goals: expressing the "True" me in each moment. Every day I go to work, I get to practice getting BIG on the inside, letting go of what is false and small and afraid. I get to practice expanding into my HUGE self. I get to practice WALKING TALL. As they say, "We teach what we most need to learn."

How to Disidentify
STEP 1: Become conscious of a pattern of experience that makes you suffer or feel small.
Example: "Every time I'm alone, I become anxious."
Or: "When I get up in front of people, I get scared they will judge me unkindly."

STEP 2: Uncover a similar pattern in your past.
Example: "I felt scared when I was left alone as a young child."
Or: "Going out in public as a kid, I was often laughed and stared at."

STEP 3: Connect your present difficulty with your past difficulty.

Example: "I was left alone as a child and felt scared. So now, when I'm alone, I feel scared."

Or: "Because I was teased excessively as a kid, I'm afraid to let people see me now."

STEP 4: See the truth for what it is.

Example: "I am now an adult who knows how to take care of myself."

Or: "Who I really am cannot be touched by the opinions of others."

STEP 5: Consciously choose to respond differently.

Example: "Instead of feeling anxious when I'm alone, I can relax."

Or: "I choose to identify with my Being, which is a perfection beyond compare."

The Role of Autonomy

When we work to break free from old identities and mental structures, a strong sense of independence and autonomy can be our best ally. If we feel we are "grown up" and self-sufficient, it's easier to let go of the "old stuff" that binds us to patterns of behavior and identities formed when we were small and dependent.

This is when doing the Monster Dance can be especially helpful because it enhances personal power and autonomy.

Let's take a look at a psychotherapy client of mine and her challenge to break free from self-criticism:

Tina was about 50 pounds overweight and very down on herself about it. We had worked with silencing her inner critic several times, but she still felt bad about herself.

In a session one day, she began an inquiry into these dynamics. She quickly recalled that, as a child, her father was very critical of himself about his weight. "I can see his attitude extended to me as well," she reported. I asked her how she felt about that. "I don't really feel much of anything," she said. I instructed, "Clench your fists slowly, first your right hand, then your left. Alternate and pay attention to the clenching." Then I had her press her feet heavily into the floor in a slow but deliberate way.

After a few minutes, I asked what she was experiencing. "I feel mad! I really hate that my dad was so critical of me. He had no right to judge me!"

I piled some pillows in front of her and told her to, "Go for it!" So she did. When she got tired and sat back, I asked how big she felt inside. "Oh, I'm as big as King Kong!" she replied in a robust voice. "From that big place inside, tell your dad how you feel about what he did."

"I'm really pissed you didn't love me as I was. I'm really angry you pushed your criticism of yourself on to me! They were YOUR critical judgments, not mine. I don't want them," she said with conviction.

I guided her to use her arms and visualize pushing his "stuff" back to him. Then I asked, "What did you get out of adopting his critical attitude?" "I got to be like him. That was a way we connected," she said. "Do you need to be connected like that with him any more?" I inquired. "No. I don't even live in the same town as he does. I can take care of myself now. I can love myself," she said.

A few months later, Tina reported she was feeling much less critical of herself. She also told me her relationship with her father had become much more harmonious. She said, "It's so amazing that allowing myself to feel my anger at him actually helped things get better between us!"

Being big energetically assisted Tina in establishing a sense of independence and autonomy. This then allowed her to break free from her childhood mental structures and let go of behaviors that no longer served her.

The Real Challenge

Intimate relationships are a particularly important

place to let go of what's false. That's because they bring up old memories and beliefs structured during our very first relationship—with our mother or primary caretaker. It's not only the good memories that get triggered, but the bad and the ugly ones, too. So, when you start to experience that merging sweetness with your lover, be aware it also stirs up memories of merging with dear-old mom. Along with the delightfulness comes the memory of frustrations, hurts, and unmet needs. This unconscious material can be a major barrier in establishing a harmonious and long-term intimate relationship.

Take my friend Mark, for example:

> Mark had been experiencing difficulties in his love relationships through most of his adult life. He had a brief reprieve, however, during the first few years of marriage. But then, a few years after the birth of their son, his wife left him for another man. Mark was bewildered over her rejection, as Mark was a mild-mannered, responsible, and caring person.
>
> A while back, Mark told me that, as a child, he often experienced great pain because his mother frequently withdrew her love from him. When his mother emotionally distanced herself, he said he felt abandoned, helpless, and scared. In response to feeling alone, Mark said he also felt angry that he

had no support and had to do everything himself.

Several years after the break up of his marriage, Mark began another intimate relationship. As he got closer to his new girlfriend, his experience was colored by the unconscious memories of merging with his mother as a child and her withdrawal. That is to say in psychological language, Mark's current romantic experience triggered an "object relationship" from the past. So, Mark reacted to his new ladylove by allowing the sweet merging, but at the same time unconsciously fearing her abandonment.

Then, despite his mild-mannered, caring demeanor, every time his girlfriend went out to enjoy her independence, it sparked Mark's memory of his mother's withdrawal. He misread her temporary move to separate as abandonment. Because he was seeing what was false and not true in the moment, Mark felt hurt and covertly acted out his insecurity. He resented her lack of support and indirectly acted out his anger every time she asked him for support.

Mark's girlfriend felt puzzled when he behaved this way and eventually she felt abused by it. His irrational insecurity and anger made her feel she had been treated unfairly. She'd get angry with him and distance herself. The rolling snowball got

> bigger and, eventually, she left him, as his wife
> did. This fulfilled Mark's expectation: "the woman
> who loves me abandons me," which was based
> on an outdated object relation.

Mark, like every other person on the face of the earth, cannot act free from the past until he becomes aware of those patterns of behavior and chooses differently. And although I have simplified this example severely, it illustrates the heart of the matter: that our *past* influences our *present* and can cause great suffering.

The difficulty is this: often the "old stuff"—the object relationships and identities—feels like an old slipper, familiar, comforting. And because we prefer the known to the unknown, we often unconsciously choose what is familiar and not what supports us most.

If Mark does not inquire into his pain of being rejected, he will continue to be instinctively drawn to women who mimic his old slipper. That means he'll naturally become interested in women who get close but then pull away—just like good ol' mom. He won't feel the same "attraction power" to someone who can love him the way he'd like to be loved: consistently. "Here today, gone to Maui." That's Mark definition of "love." And that is what he'll automatically go after.

Remember my story about Dale from England? Same thing. I was attracted to what was *familiar* (love and rejection), not what was healthy. So beware! The person who seems to attract you the most might not necessarily be the one you will have an easy, satisfying relationship with. Intensity of attraction is more often about issues needing resolution than about "love."

Disidentifying with past object relations is a major step in the right direction for creating a better future. The more you know the truth of who you are, the more readily you can let go of any false identities as they arise. The more you think, speak, and act from the truth of your Being, the more your life will be filled with love and joy.

BE THAT MAGNIFICENCE!

> " *The privilege of a life time is being who you are.* "
>
> —JOSEPH CAMPBELL

Once you unveil the diamond within and let go of what is false, you will be WALKING TALL quite naturally. The challenge now will be to not revert to that small little person inside every time *you* meet with difficulty and failure. The challenge now will be to embody your magnificent self, express your inherent greatness, and let others see the glory of you!

There is a difference between being "big" by virtue of the personality and being "big" by virtue of your essence. The ego personality, founded in greed and inadequacy, seeks only to hide the inadequacy and acquire whatever it can. **But being "big" from the perspective of essence is about letting the glories inside of you come out. It's about the simple, natural expression of who you truly are.** It's not for pretense; it's not for show. It's just the natural movement of your Big Self fulfilling its potential.

So, unveil the diamond inside of you. Let that diamond shimmer and glow. Let out the brilliance. Let your whole self radiate with the magnificence that you are. Be BIG! Be HUGE! Be GIGANTIC and WALK TALL!

PART THREE
CONCLUSION

Slowing down, inquiring into the truth, and meditating can all help shift your attention inward and create a balance between your inner and outer life. This balance can add a dimension to human experience that is otherwise empty and meaningless. It takes a person of BIG character to break away from the mainstream culture; to develop and practice the disciplines needed to nurture an inner life. Once you see the depths of you and unveil your diamond within, you will effortlessly exude your innate magnificence. WALKING TALL is a natural outcome. So, quiet down and peek inside.

PART FOUR

CELEBRATING
YOUR
UNIQUENESS

INTRO:
SNOWFLAKES

A boundless blanket of snow covers Arctic regions, thousands of square miles of white terrain. Fresh fleeting flurries fall almost every day. Every flake of snow is one of a kind, each with an individual design, its own matchless pattern. Who isn't in awe of such a profound phenomenon?

> "
> *No other person in the world is quite like you, and no other person can give what you have to give. So, don't give up. Just by being you, you are a blessing to the world!*
> "
>
> —Unknown

Across the globe people travel to see natural wonders. They flock to zoos, botanical gardens, natural history museums, arboretums, as well as wildlife and national parks to experience the magnificent diversity of our natural world.

People celebrate diversity in nature. Interesting, then, how they often tend to scorn differences among their own species. They ask: Is this the right weight, the right height, the right complexion, the right nose, hair, lips, hands, and so on. Are others "just like us?" Do they measure up? Aren't our people better than their people?

Celebrating uniqueness among humankind has certainly undergone some healthy changes over the last few centuries. Still, won't it be a wonderfully different world when human beings exude the same enthusiasm for differences among people as they do for differences in nature?

❶

HEALTHY
PRIDE

> "
> *Every woman
> has something
> beautiful she can
> celebrate about
> herself, beginning
> on the inside*
> "
>
> —OPRAH WINFREY

Healthy pride is the pride that allows you to feel good about yourself—pleased, dignified, even bold. Healthy pride is like confidence, only more centering, more loving, more personal. Healthy pride provides the sense that you love yourself just the way you are. You not only love yourself, but you respect and cherish yourself. It's natural. It's relaxed. It's not boastful or loud. It is a gentle presence, a substantial internal support that flows from your essence and allows you to WALK TALL.

LOVE WHO YOU ARE

I went to Oregon one weekend several years ago to visit my friends Linda and Tim. They are both massage therapists and psychotherapists. One afternoon, Tim gave me a back massage. As he was finishing, his wife Linda quietly came into the room. She sat down and greeted me with smiling eyes. She looked at my hand lying on the table and, from the look on her face, I could see her recounting a conversation we had had the previous day.

> *Happiness is feeling good about yourself*
>
> —LOUISE L. HAYES

I had shared with her something I rarely talk about—how I **really** feel about my hands. I told her what a difficult time I had trying to accept them. "They have always been laughed at, made fun of," I told her. "They have limited me incredibly. I can't do anything that requires gripping or squeezing. My fingers are so squat and unfeminine. They're so ugly, so fat and pudgy. I just can't imagine ever being able to love these hands," I said with a sense of defeat.

As I lay on the massage table, Linda took my hands in hers. She closed her eyes and took a deep breath. She asked me to close my eyes and imagine light streaming into my body's center, then to move the light out from my center to my extremities.

When the light reached my hands, I felt the

warmth. Linda then asked me to list all the things my hands do for me. I said, "Well, let's see. I use my hands for holding my fork and spoon while I eat. I use them to wash my body, do the dishes, load the laundry." I thought for a moment. "I use them to write, type, draw, and dial the phone. They hold the steering wheel when I drive. They pick flowers, cut vegetables, turn pages, apply make-up, itch my itches. My hands do an amazing number of things for me!" I enthused. Over the next few minutes as I was lying there, I noticed what a difference "shifting my focus" had made. I shifted my attention off of what's wrong about my hands, and on to what's right about them.

> "
> Insomuch as love grows in you, so in you beauty grows. For love is the beauty of the soul."
> "
>
> —St. Augustine

Linda spoke softly, saying, "Every day, take a few minutes and focus on your hands. Appreciate what your hands do for you. Be grateful for the miracle in them. Surround your hands with light and bow to them. Honor them. They are special and talented friends."

Since that time, I have practiced that meditation almost daily. I have gradually melted away

> the old beliefs and feelings about my hands being
> "ugly." I have learned to appreciate them, accept
> them, love them, even take pride in their unique-
> ness. This has been a giant step for me in learn-
> ing how to love who I am.

Many people, not only me, suffer because they don't "fit" the cultural picture that defines success, beauty, wealth, and so on. Many tend to focus on and even obsess about how they don't match up or how they aren't good enough. This self-criticism and self-loathing is a fountainhead of inner smallness.

Loving who you are can be challenging for many reasons.

First, we know ourselves by how others respond to us. As children, we gain our sense of "self" by how our family greets us, responds to our various needs, and welcomes us into each situation.

Did you get the message back then that you were celebrated? wonderful? perfect in every way? important? Were your needs responded to with joy? If so, you are fortunate; you were seen in the light of truth. For those who did not receive this response, you got messages about who you were and your worth that were not so positive. As a result, it will be more challenging for you to love and accept yourself as you are now.

Second, we learn about the world and ourselves through discrimination—through discerning differences like white or black, tall or small, slow or quick. This process lends itself to a lot of comparing. "Am I as

_____ as her/him?" Certainly we all have different strengths and weaknesses. Often when we compare ourselves to others, we focus on what they do or what they have that is better than us. We often totally overlook the incredible gifts of our own specialties.

Third, the media constantly bombards us with images of the "ideal." These incessant images penetrate into our cultural awareness. We are programmed to measure everything against these standards. Few of us look as good when held up against the airbrushed magazine model, Hollywood superstar, or champion athlete.

Fourth, growing up in an environment of criticism adds another difficulty. Many times, family or community members focus on what they consider to be our quirks, limitations, and weaknesses, rather than our strengths and assets. We internalize their negative messages and, today, see ourselves through the same critical glasses.

Some people's flaws are easier to see than others. Yet, whether readily observable or not, every person alive has some imperfection. Since this is a universal condition, know that you are not alone in this department.

Accepting yourself as you are—loving who you are— is difficult work because of these factors that pose challenges. Yet, working through and overcoming them leads to feeling and expressing confidence, to being happy and at peace, and to enjoying life to the fullest.

Do you consider loving who you are an act of conceit or self-righteousness? On the contrary, loving who you are is an act of incredible courage and compassion. It means you accept yourself as you are, despite others' opinions, despite your flaws and imperfections. That takes incredible courage, and incredible compassion.

Loving who you are means appreciating your strong points and your wins, plus accepting the things that aren't so perfect. People who love who they are take good care of themselves and treat themselves with the same kindness, honor, and respect with which they treat their loved ones. By loving themselves first, they are so much better equipped to love others.

People who love themselves are BIG inside. They know they may be flawed on the surface but, deep down, are precious beyond compare. They embody their diamond within, hold their heads high, treat themselves kindly, then others follow suit.

If you love yourself, others will love you, too. But if you don't love yourself, it doesn't matter how much they love you. You'll never believe or feel their love; you'll never allow yourself to absorb it. So, be the first one on your block to love who you are!

STAND UP STRAIGHT

To exude the inner qualities of WALKING TALL, express them in the most obvious thing about you: your body language. Standing up straight communicates to yourself and others that, "I'm here. I matter. I respect myself. I'm sure of myself. I'm powerful. I'm open to meet you. I feel good

> "
> *How we stand says something not just about us, but to us.*
> "
>
> —GLORIA STEINEM

about myself." These are very potent messages.

Stand straight with a tall spine and erect head, even if you're taller than most of the people around you. Hold your head high. Fill your chest with big breaths. When you speak to someone, look at his or her face, allow eye contact. Show that you value what you have to say by sharing your thoughts. Speak clearly and loud enough so others can hear you. Listen attentively when people speak. When you shake someone's hand, do it with firmness and sincerity. Be present. Dress in a manner that is tasteful, stylish, and non-offensive to others. Smile when you greet people. Smile when you're happy.

Part of WALKING TALL is letting the world know you feel good about yourself, that you have confidence in yourself. To WALK TALL, exude your inner power and might, your joyful and compassionate heart. Adopting this posture can support these qualities as they develop inside of you. Even if you don't feel 100% proud of yourself yet, keep standing straight and WALKING TALL!

❷

DIFFERENCES ARE
A GOOD THING

CELEBRATE DIFFERENCES

Birthdays were always a big deal in our home. That's because my mom loved to celebrate and always made a big hoopla on that special day. When Mom gave a birthday party, she went ALL OUT! My friends loved to come to our house because they considered our parties to be the best—we had the best games and the best cake and the best ice cream. I especially loved my own birthday parties because we came together to celebrate my uniqueness.

Back in the early '60s, it was customary to wear a "party dress" and fancy shoes to birthday parties. But when I was about to turn eight, I wanted to have an outdoor party and have everybody play outdoor games. I told my mom, "To play all these games, we are going to get all messy. Can't we ask my friends to wear play clothes instead of party clothes?" My mom said no problem. I'm sure my pals still remember that "shorts and T-shirts" birthday party. It revolutionized party attire for all the kids in my circle from that day on.

The following year, when I was nine, my mom asked me what I wanted for my birthday present. I told her I wanted a pet. "What kind of pet? A puppy, a kitten, or a bird?" she asked. I answered, "None of those, Mom. I want a baby lamb." She may have suspected this answer since I was focused on lambs in a big way at the time. She just smiled and said, "Don't get your hopes up."

The morning of my birthday came. My mom brought me breakfast in bed with all my favorite foods, as she always did on my special day. I opened all my presents, but no baby lamb. When we went to get in the car

to go to school, I felt a little disappointed. Then I looked in our yard and saw the most precious, soft, white little lamb ever! It was love at first sight. We immediately named her Sugar.

Later that afternoon, my mom brought Sugar to school along with homemade cupcakes for all my classmates. They all sang, "Peggy had a little lamb..." Thanks, Mom! You sure made me feel special by using your talents to celebrate my uniqueness!

KEEP AN OPEN MIND & AN OPEN HEART

Have you ever known people who behave like they're wearing horse blinders? (These blinders are flaps placed on the bridle next to a horse's eyes. They keep the horse from seeing anything but a narrow path straight ahead.) Have you ever known someone who didn't want to move forward, didn't want to change, didn't want to learn anything new? Ever met someone who didn't respect people with a different set of values, beliefs or cultural rituals? Have you ever known folks who make up their minds and will not budge from their positions, no matter what? I have. These shut-down folks are wrought with inner smallness.

When I speak to children in elementary schools. I start with, "Presenters may come to your assemblies and talk to you about eating your vegetables so you can get big on the OUTside. But today, we're going to be talking about getting big in another way: getting big on the INside."

I continue by saying, "What does it mean to be BIG on

the inside? It means having an open mind and a big heart. It means being kind to everyone. People who are BIG on the inside celebrate their own uniqueness and honor the differences

in others." It's amazing that even five year olds have no difficulty understanding my description of a person with a BIG character.

When your mind is open, you are able to easily take in new ideas, new information, and new ways of doing things. You are available to absorb your moment-to-moment experiences. With an open mind, change is simply a part of life and does not necessarily pose a threat.

An open heart lets you feel connected to what is happening around you. Not just in your immediate environment, but to all people and to the planet itself. An open heart allows you to feel compassion. This openness can unlock the door to new friendships, new adventures, and new places. It can support a deepening into established relationships and provide greater insight into your experiences.

Keeping an open heart requires staying emotionally present and vulnerable. To keep an open mind, you must be willing to let go of your fears, whatever they may be. You can see that keeping an open mind and heart is no small order. It takes a great bravery to remain open to change. So, be BIG. Be brave. And open up to all the goodness around you!

HONOR THE UNIQUENESS IN ALL BEINGS

At the end of my year studying with my dance teacher Anna, we held a performance for the people in our vicinity. Through the performance, we wanted to honor our local nature deity—Mount Tamalpias.

Anna had envisioned showing the audience the "spirit" of the mountain, but how could we accomplish that ethereal task?

Here's what we did. At the end of the presentation, all the dancers clustered in a circle. They stretched their arms upward and inward to form the mountain. I was squashed down in the middle where no one in the audience could see me. Then, magically, I appeared at the summit of the mountain, hovering above it under a single spotlight. There I was, the spirit of the mountain. In this dance, my difference in stature not only presented a solution; it honored me and my differences at the same time.

Encountering people who are different from us can sometimes be worrisome. We can never be sure how people from a distant land or with different values or abilities may respond in any given situation. They might be kind, or they might be aggressive. We might do something unknowingly that hurts or offends them. As a species, we innately feel leery when we run into the unknown, when we meet someone from outside of our day-to-day life.

From watching my dogs make friends with new dogs, I'm intrigued to notice that the first issue they work out is who will be the top dog. It seems to me that humans are governed by similar instincts.

It takes a person of BIG character to override these "top dog" instincts based in fear. It takes inner BIGness to see what is true in the moment and to sense whether the person you're dealing with feels safe or not. It takes courage to open your minds and hearts, to let go of your preference for what's familiar. It takes curiosity to find out what others who differ from you think and value. It takes love to share with others, putting aside any impulse to dominate. All these things require us to be BIG inside, and nurture our inner BIGness, as well.

Just because others have different religions, preferences, or points of view doesn't mean you have to convert to their way. It doesn't require you to agree with them. Honoring others means respecting them, treating them with courtesy and kindness. It means listening to others without trying to change them, sharing with others without having to be right. *Enjoy* the differences among people! See them as spices of life, as flavors of fun!

Differences among people bring a potential for conflict, but also a possibility for increased *"solution power."* A group of folks from a variety of backgrounds and orientations have a great advantage in tackling problems. In any think tank, they will be able to offer a higher number of resolutions. So, shift your attention off of the potential conflict and onto the emergence of greater creativity and intelligence.

My angle on diversity is to assist people in learning how to love and honor themselves. This includes coming to terms with their own shortcomings. As we develop compassion and understanding for our own imperfections and limitations, we develop the ability to extend these sentiments to others. When you accept yourself, accepting differences in others is no problem.

Every person has a diamond inside. Every human being is intrinsically valuable. Everyone deserves respect. No matter where people come from, no matter the color of their skin, or their level of education. No matter what they believe in, their age, their economic status, or their level of self-sufficiency. Everyone deserves respect.

EXERCISE How open am I?

1. While you stand in line at the bank, wait for a bus or an airplane, or just sit on a park bench, notice what happens inside as you watch people walk by. What does your internal dialogue sound like? Is it critical and fearful, or accepting and open? Just tune in and notice. Write a paragraph in your journal about your self-observation.
2. Would you like to increase your capacity to honor the differences in others? How might you accomplish this? Make a plan and implement it.

EXERCISE　Honoring Hoe-down

In your journal, answer these questions as thoroughly and honestly as possible:

1. What part of you do you consider unique or different? How have you responded to that part of yourself in the past? Now?

2. What part of you do others consider unique or different? How have they responded to that in the past? Now?

3. Were you ever teased for being or looking different in some way? Do you still get down on yourself for the same thing? If so, how frequently?

4. List at least 10 ways you could honor your own uniqueness.

5. How would you rate your capacity for honoring the uniqueness in:

    a. your spouse or partner?

    b. each of your children?

    c. your closest co-worker?

    d. your best friend?

    e. your parents and siblings?

6. How do they know you honor them? What specific behaviors or words do you use?

7. If you wanted to improve your capacity in honoring the uniqueness of others, what might you do? What impact do you think that might have on them?

Do these two exercises again in a month and see what has changed. Repeat as often as you like.

BE UNIQUE AND FIT IN, TOO

I first learned about celebrating my uniqueness from my friend Eeo, the one who snagged me into going to Anna's "dance" workshop. Eeo is an extraordinary human being, truly one of a kind! Eeo is an artist—creative and distinctly unique in her dress, her home, her artwork, her style of relating, her preferences, and even her sense of humor. They all reflect a flare of reckless abandon, of celebration, of pure creative expression.

It's not that she doesn't care what others think. It's that she's more concerned with being true to herself than in pledging allegiance to others. Eeo reveres her individuality. She takes pride in her outlandish mannerisms, in her avant-garde style. Skillful in breaking free from conventionality, she has allowed herself a freedom that is rarely matched. Not everyone understands her. But everyone is tickled by and in awe of her sense of profound individualism.

Eeo has always supported me in letting go of trying to be like others. She showed me how to

From "Still Dances" by Eeo and me

celebrate my unique size, whether I liked it or not. The road was long and hard, but eventually I got the message. In time, I understood that trying to fit the mold simply made me miserable. Only when I found the courage to break free and celebrate my "shortcomings," did I begin to feel truly happy.

We all want to be our own person and, at the same time, we all want to feel connected to others. Individual but unified. How is that possible?

At all levels of human development, this dichotomy goes on. As toddlers, as teens, as adults, we fight for our independence but also strive to stay connected at the same time.

This process only poses a conflict for people wrought with inner smallness. These folks feel insecure because they believe they are less than others. The efforts of their personality, then, are to conform or please others so they can win the love and attention they feel unworthy of. Their expressions of self then feel forced and contrived.

As a result, these types of behaviors fail to invite easy connection or lasting relationships; people are drawn to what they discern to be genuine.

By contrast, when people relax about who they are, accept their own quirks, and express their uniqueness without questioning "Am I acceptable or not," they have a much easier time fitting in.

I'm not saying that if you swing from the chandeliers

everyone will go crazy over you. Just be aware there's a difference between authentically expressing your uniqueness and showing off to get attention. A big difference.

Some people think that because they look different or come from a different background they have to follow certain rules so they can "fit in." If that's true for you, turning to your inner guidance for support can help you to act appropriately in differing situations. But I believe the more you let your uniqueness shine, the more ease you will have connecting with others.

Here's what happened when I let my uniqueness shine:

As I ventured into the marketplace in my prior careers as a photographer and as a psychothera-pist, I considered my short stature a detriment, not a benefit. Back then, I was fearful that if I put myself "out there," people would be afraid of my different form and/or would judge me as being inadequate. I thought if people knew I was a Little Person, I'd be less likely to get business. First I believed that state-

ment; then, as always, I created the reality to match my belief.

By the time I became a speaker-author, however, I had learned to appreciate my uniqueness and saw it as my greatest asset. The best thing about being three-and-a-half-feet tall is that people remember me. Now I use this shortcoming as my central selling point and main marketing strategy. I've done a full "180."

My promo photos are now designed to capitalize on my uniqueness. The titles of my programs, as well as the title of this book, all play off my diminutive stature. My copy for articles and publications mention something about my height in the first sentence. When I call people on the phone, I mention my size within the first few minutes. I know others don't meet Little People every day, and that, for me, is a HUGE advantage!

I've let go of seeing myself through the eyes of conventionality, the eyes of prejudice, the eyes of fear. Now, I walk proudly, with dignity.

We cannot help but be unique. There is no one else like ourself and that is the wonderful thing to discover and uncover. So uniqueness is not only about being different. It is about being our true self, as well as our highest spiritual self, and that is where the work comes in.

EXERCISE Celebrate Your Uniqueness

1. In your journal, answer these questions:
   • What's unique about you?
   • What's your opinion, belief, feeling about your uniqueness?
   • What are the limitations your uniqueness puts on you?
   • What are the advantages of your uniqueness?
   • Do you try to hide what is unique about you? How?
   • Do you use your uniqueness to your advantage? How?
2. Are there circumstances in which your uniqueness would be more of a benefit than a detriment? If so, list them and make a plan to accentuate them.

SHINE

Celebrating your uniqueness is about rejoicing in what is different about you. It's about showing the world who you are with pride and joy. It's about sharing your gifts and talents with those around you. Differences are the glory of this creation! So let yours SHINE!

DO WHAT YOU'RE GOOD AT

What are you good at doing? Perhaps your forté is in sports, science, or art. Perhaps you're an outstanding organizer, inventor, or chef. Maybe you're great at singing, gardening, or writing. Everyone is good at something. It doesn't have to be a major career to count as being good. Perhaps what you do best is smile and give encouragement. Maybe you're great at listening or being a

> "
> *Live your life so that when you sing your death song, you will die like a hero who is going home with no shame to meet the Creator and your family.*
> "
> —TECUMSEH, CHIEF OF THE SHAWNEE NATION

compassionate friend. Remember, simply being present is something everyone can do and that is one of the greatest gifts you can give.

First identify what you're good at, and then focus on developing your unique talents. Apply yourself. Invest time and energy and resources needed to develop those gifts. If you need more training, sign up for a class or workshop. Ask experts to teach you. As author Joseph Campbell advised, "Follow your bliss."

Sometimes it's challenging to follow your bliss, given social pressure to conform. If others feel uncomfortable when you shine, invite them to join you in celebrating your uniqueness.

You may encounter obstacles in developing your talents. You may lack opportunities, finances, support, or other resources. When that's the case, you must seek alternative methods, creative methods, to gather the resources you need. Find a way around the roadblock. Keep the goal alive in your heart. And persist!

Sometimes it's hard to identify what you are good at; you simply just don't know. In that case, ask yourself, "What do I do that really makes me feel alive? What's easy for me?" If you're still clueless, start doing things you've never done before. Try different creative ventures like playing diverse musical instruments or drawing with a variety of mediums such as paint, pastels, or pencils. If you're athletically inclined, play new sports. If you're good with people, volunteer for a variety of groups. Read books on topics of your personal interests. Pay attention to what comes easily and what you enjoy.

Expand outside your box. Be BIG. Explore.

Identify what you are good at, apply hard work, and develop your skills. Then you will have something unique, something marvelous, something all your own to enjoy and offer to those around you.

> During my life, I found many things that I'm good at. As a kid, I was an accomplished ice skater. As a teen, I found I had talent as a photographer and eventually went to school to become a professional. While I was working out a lot of my personal problems, I discovered I had a knack for psychotherapy and assisting others toward well-being. Out of that, I recognized I was gifted in my ability to articulate. That was the impetus for becoming an inspirational speaker, which then expanded to becoming an author.

There's no limit to the number of things you can be good at and enjoy doing. Find out what yours are and, as my speaker friend Larry Winget says, "Exploit your uniqueness in the service of others."

If you can earn an income doing what you're good at, all the better. Find out what the going rate is for your service. Let lots of people know about what you have to offer. Market yourself big time! Let your talents shine and enjoy the process.

SHARE YOUR TALENTS
WITH THE WORLD

The Bible says, "Don't hide a lantern under a basket." In other words, don't hide your talents. Share them. Let them enlighten and warm others. Let them be a gift. Let them be enjoyed!

Putting yourself "out there" can be frightening, however. Being seen can be upsetting. Someone might judge you. Someone might not like you or what you do. Then what?

WALKING TALL means overcoming these fearful notions and letting your brilliance shimmer. Encourage yourself. Value yourself and what you do. Make mistakes. Receive feedback. Work hard and excel. If you falter, get up and try again. Build a support system. Ask for help. Do some therapy. Get a coach. All of these things can help you take your unique talents and share them with those around you.

Here's a story about celebrating my uniqueness with those around me:

> *When my time is up, and I stand before my maker, I'd like to be able to say 'God, I don't have one ounce of talent, love compassion or energy left. I used every gift you gave me.'*
>
> —MONTEL WILLIAMS

> I told you about my skating friend Allison, who was a slender 5 foot 8 inches. No two figures at our rink were more different than hers and mine. Well, we were so tickled by our physical differ-

ences that one day we decided to enter a skating competition in the "pairs" events.

Usually pairs are well suited to one another such as my cousins, identical twins, who we competed against. But not Allison and me; we capitalized on our contrary statures!

Instead of doing tricks in unison, we did moves that exploited our differences. When my pal Al would do a spin with her leg up behind her (a camel spin), instead of doing one in the usual manner next to her, I'd do a Russian jig around her spinning leg while her other skate whirled wildly above my head. Instead of doing a spread eagle (gliding sideways with both feet turned out) side by side, she'd do a spread eagle crossing the rink from left to right, then I'd head her off at a perpendicular angle and shoot-the-duck through her legs. Most all our stunts were custom made and definitely wowed the crowd!

We were lucky to win a few competitions. In some cases, I'm not sure we won because we were the strongest skaters. I am sure, however, that we did the best in turning a disadvantage into an advantage and at bringing a smile of surprise to everyone there.

Approached with the right attitude, celebrating your

uniqueness can be the thing that "wows" your crowd. So share your unique talents with the people around you and let yourself SHINE!

EXERCISE   **What's right about staying small?**

This exercise is to be done as a "repeating question." A repeating question is when you answer the same question over and over again. The repetition draws you into deeper levels of your subconscious mind. You can do this exercise with a friend or by writing a list of answers as you ask yourself the question repeatedly. When you work with a partner there are a few guidelines:

Appoint a speaker and a questioner. The questioner will direct the question to the speaker (with the exact same words) and then listen attentively to the response. When the speaker is done talking, acknowledge their answer by saying thank you. Then ask the question again. No commentary is permitted from the questioner. After ten or fifteen minutes of asking the question, you can switch roles.

When you are asked in a repeating question what's right about something, it means what is the payoff? What's the advantage you get from this behavior? For example:

Q.: What's right about staying small?
A. I get to be safe.
Thank you.

> Q.: What's right about staying small?
> A. I can take it easy because I have no responsibilities.
> Thank you.
>
> Q.: What's right about staying small?
> A. Someone else will take care of me.
> Thank you.

(Thus you reveal to yourself the payoffs you get for behaviors you may consciously consider undesirable.)

EXERCISE Monologue:
If I had no fear

Speak for 15 minutes on each of these questions to a partner. The questioner asks the question and then listens attentively for the allotted time without speaking. The speaker talks on this topic for the entire time. Then switch roles. If you don't have someone to work with, you can do this in your journal. Write a half page or more on each of these questions:

• How much does the fear of being seen or judged hold me back from freely expressing my talents?

• If I had no fear, what would I be doing with my life?

• How could I better share my talents with the world?

PART FOUR
CONCLUSION

Won't it be a wonderful world when the differences among people are revered with the same enthusiasm as the differences among trees and flowers? To get there we must celebrate differences! We must not only feel good about ourselves, but also cherish our uniqueness and share our special talents with the world. We must stand up straight and show the world how much we love ourselves. We must keep an open mind and heart to the differences in others. We have to be brave and let go of our fearful notions about people who are different from us. Differences are the glory of this creation! Celebrate your uniqueness and honor the differences in others! Then you will be well on your way to WALKING TALL!

PART FIVE

EXPANDING
INTO YOUR
HUGE SELF

INTRO:
LET YOURSELF
BE HUGE!

Expansion just feels *good*. Taking a deep breath, freely expressing what's inside, being seen, achieving goals, deepening love, gaining knowledge, strengthening your connection to God, becoming empowered, enhancing physical strength, influencing others, increasing income, getting to know your True Nature—

> "
> *One can never
> consent to creep
> when one feels an
> impulse to soar.*
> "
>
> —HELEN KELLER

all these things are part of getting HUGE and being HUGE. And they all feel *great*!

As kids, many of us were reprimanded for expressing ourselves boldly. We were taught it was impolite, even rude. We were warned about looking conceited, being too loud, or taking up too much space. Sadly, many of us pulled in the reins on our self-expression and sought instead to be quiet, small, and soft-spoken.

WALKING TALL requires us to break free from any fearful notions that "dwarf" us. We must allow ourselves to take up space—both physically and energetically—to be empowered, to know, to do, to have, and to lead.

Expanding into your HUGE self is about giving yourself permission to be big, huge, gigantic! It's not just about integrating the qualities of inner BIGness. It's about *embodying* them, living them! Then you get to fully enjoy your expansion and the world gets the benefit of your loving influence and wise leadership. So, go ahead and give yourself permission to be HUGE inside, and see how fabulous it feels!

❶

VIBE
INFECTIOUS JOY

Being happy is part of WALKING TALL. Let that joy inside spill over so it uplifts those around you. Smile when you are happy! Let your face glow, your eyes twinkle, and your grin widen as you greet others. Share your jubilation.

"
Whoever is happy will make others happy too.
"
—Anne Frank

Babies laughing. This is the quintessential source of infectious joy. When you get around babies, you just feel happy. Their joy draws you in. You want to get close, tickle them, make them giggle, hold them. You want what they have—a direct line to internal bliss. Certainly, they go in and out of bliss at a rapid rate. Nonetheless, babies freely show their elation to everything that makes them happy. And you feel gladdened by it!

Babies are good teachers in that respect. If only we all could let out what we feel so easily, without worry of being judged or misunderstood, the world would be a sunnier, funnier place.

Having some fun now!

So, express your joy freely. Let others witness your glee. Greet people with a warm embrace. Say something nice. Give them a compliment. Acknowledge them. Tell funny stories. Tell jokes. Laugh. Be uplifting.

By vibing infectious joy, you can uplift sunken spirits, turn a smile, inspire hope, make someone's day, and maybe even change someone's life. So, next time you feel like jumping up and clicking your heels together, don't hold back. Just do it!

TAKE RISKS

When my husband Brad gets in water, he sinks to the bottom. He also has a small rib cage that restricts the expansion of his lungs. When he breathes in, he only gets 60% of the oxygen most people get. So doing any activity that requires stamina is not really possible for him. Put these things together and you have a person who cannot swim.

When Brad and I went to Hawaii a few years ago, I knew he couldn't swim. What I didn't know, however, was that he had almost drowned on three different occasions and had to be yanked out of the water.

> "
> *Far better it is to dare mighty things, to win glorious triumphs, even though checkered by failure, than to rank with those poor spirits who neither suffer much nor enjoy much because they live in the gray twilight that knows neither victory nor defeat.*
> "
>
> —TEDDY ROOSEVELT

On our first trip to my old hometown of Kona, I wanted Brad to enjoy one of my very favorite activities—swimming with the dolphins down at Kealakekua Bay. Brad was quite eager to join me, but because the bay was large, we had to make provisions for Brad to float.

We drove down the winding road to the bay in anxious anticipation that we would soon meet some dolphins in the wild. At the water's edge, we put on our snorkel gear. Brad also sported an inflatable scuba vest. (We tested it in our friend's pool to make sure it would keep him afloat.) At that place, we had to enter the ocean from a lava rock shore. The water was calm that day, so getting in was no problem.

Brad and I waded into the warm water and began our swim into the bay. I was concerned for him, but he seemed to trust the vest to hold him up. After we got a ways out, however, there was a problem. His vest was inflated in the front. In the pool, this arrangement seemed to work just fine, keeping him afloat, and all. But swimming a distance was very different. The front air pockets kept turning him over on his back as he swam. Between struggling to keep his snorkel and mask in the water and all the flutter kicking, Brad got exhausted. So we turned back.

We returned to the beach a few days later, now

equipped with a boogie board in place of the scuba vest. The entry conditions were less than ideal; white water was splashing up on the rocks. But we decided to make a go for it.

We put on our snorkeling gear and stood at the edge of the water watching the pattern of waves. We had to be careful because we needed to pass through a lava rock gateway to enter the bay. When things calmed down a bit, Brad hopped onto his boogie board and started kicking like mad. He passed through the gate without any problems. I followed behind hm.

We started to meander out into the big blue bay that was at least a mile wide and about 60 feet deep. Brad was a champ! He stayed calm and didn't seem the least bit concerned that he was heading out into the ocean and couldn't swim. As we snorkeled out farther, I told Brad we had to keep our eye out for the dolphins. Once we made our way toward the middle of the bay, Brad said, "Let me call the dolphins. Let's see if I can get them to come to us." I said, "Fine" but thought "Yeah, right!" So Brad began his ritual of tapping the water's surface ever so slightly and gently calling for our sea-friends. He had no more energy to swim on, so we waited in that place patiently.

After 10 minutes or so, I looked down and saw three curious dolphins circling beneath us. They *slowly swam on and we followed behind for as long as Brad could go. We stopped again to rest. Just a few moments later, dorsal fins approached us. We looked down and saw a whole pod of dolphins, at least 30 of them. We swam and danced, Brad still on his boogie board. We mimicked their frolicking movements, thoroughly enjoying the enchanting encounter.*

After a while, they ventured off into the wild blue yonder. We waved good-bye and began our snorkel back to shore. We climbed up on the warm black beach rocks and sat there awhile, fully content. We looked at each other, our smiles spread from ear to ear. We knew this little ocean adventure would stand out as a highlight in our life together.

Brad really took a risk! He expanded into his HUGE self. He summoned his courage and faith and said, "I *want* to do this. I *can* do this!" Brad showed incredible bravery at Kealakekua Bay. And it didn't end there. His love for the ocean and his ocean pals has taken him into the deep many times since.

Yes, Brad entered the water and wrestled with his disability. He faced his fear time and again. He developed his skill and eventually overcame his challenge. Now Brad can swim. Bravo Brad!

What fears are holding you back from doing what you want to do, going after what you want, or being who you want to be? What risks could you take to face those fears and overcome them?

Be BIG. Be courageous! Take risks! And expand some more!

EXERCISE   **Attitude Aptitude**

Write a paragraph in your journal on two or three risks you have taken in your life and the outcome of those experiences.

Then write an answer to these questions:
- What was your basic attitude about taking risks then?
- What is your attitude about taking a risk to expand you, your life or your capacities now?
- Does your attitude about taking risks need an adjustment? If so, what can you do to make your attitude more optimistic?

EXERCISE   **Risky Business**

Write the answers to these questions:
- What have I been really wanting to do or be, but have not accomplished yet?
- Is there some risk I need to take to accomplish this goal? If yes, what is it?
- What are the barriers I have to taking this risk?
- If I take it, what are the possible outcomes, positive and negative?
- What can I gain from the experience?

If you decide to take the risk, make a plan. Create step 1, 2, and so on. Then implement it.

❸

ASK FOR
WHAT YOU WANT

Four things are required to ask for what you want:
1. You are clear about what you want.
2. You believe you are worthy of having it.
3. You believe you will get it.
4. You are bold enough to speak up about it.

Asking for what you want is a powerful technique for bringing about positive change in your life. It allows you to dream a dream as BIG as you can, then ask others for support as you work to manifest that dream. It allows you to share your dreams with others and make them part of it.

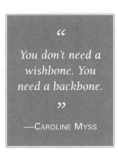

You don't need a wishbone. You need a backbone.

—CAROLINE MYSS

Asking for what you want exercises your power to

create. Your spoken word is very powerful indeed. With your words, you create great impact—positive or negative. You bring what does not yet exist into existence. That's power! When you use your words to express your wishes, you plant seeds for bringing those desires into reality.

Who do you ask for what you want? You can ask God, yourself, the universe, a friend, your parents, your family members, experts, people with great resources, or a stranger. You can ask just about anybody for what you want, but who you *select* to ask is very important. No need to build frustration by asking a lot of people who will probably say "no." Instead, direct your request to those most likely to say "yes" and are able to fulfill it.

Be as precise as possible in asking for what you want. Sort through your many ideas and wishes. Get crystal clear on what you desire. You could make a written list to help you clarify your priorities. Then simplify and strengthen your language. When asking for what you want, make sure you say what you intend as clearly and succinctly as possible.

Part of having the confidence to ask for what you want is believing you are worthy of receiving it. If *you* believe you are worthy, whoever hears your words will pick up on your conviction and be much more apt to fulfill your request. If they feel your self-doubt, winning them over will pose more of a challenge.

Believe it's possible to get what you ask for. Remember that your beliefs create your reality. So before wasting a lot of time gathering support to make your dreams come true, make sure you believe you can actually pull it off—and sustain it.

Once all this is in order, you will have the confidence to ask directly for what you want. It not only serves you; it serves others as well. People can't read your mind. Most people would love to help you make your dreams come true. When they know specifically how they can support you, you conserve their energy from guessing. And you let them know you honor them by including them in your plan.

You can ask for anything you want—BIG or small. It can be a chocolate chip ice cream cone or a country estate. You can ask someone to lend a hand to reach something, or you can simply ask someone to believe in you. In every case, express your all-powerful words with confidence. Be BIG! Be bold! Ask for what you want!

4

LAUGH
AT YOURSELF

When I saw Brad for the first time, I was immediately attracted to his long thick hair and eyelashes that seemed to touch the sky. The fateful night when I met him, the Little People's convention week was nearly half over. I knew I had to work fast! So, I put him through

"Peggy's instant attitude test." In our first conversation I asked him, "Why are you a Little Person?" "Whaaaat?" he replied. "Why are you a Little Person?" I repeated. "Well, you see before I was born, God gave me a choice. He said I could be tall or I could have great hair!"

Brad's humorous response was the green light that turned my deeper attention to him. Over my many years at LPA conventions, I had asked that question to size up several Little People. I was usually met with answers like, "Because God was in a bad mood the day I was born." Brad's ability to laugh at himself let me know he had a positive attitude about his situation. That was the real "go" sign for me. The rest, as you know, is history.

Use self-deprecating humor, giggle at your failures, be the brunt of the joke, let others see you don't take yourself too seriously, find the humor in everything about yourself—even when you make a huge mistake like I did:

It was a crisp fall Thursday afternoon in Iowa. I walked into the college cafeteria to get my lunch and sat down with a new group of fellow students. They were all talking about cutting out of philosophy class that afternoon and taking a little road trip. Next thing I knew, I was in my ol' beat-up cowboy hat zooming westward on the highway, headed for Boulder, Colorado.

Now, I had had an extended stay in Boulder just a year before. My best friend from grade school, Mary, lived there and went to the

University of Colorado. I had stayed with her for several weeks while I did some apprenticing—teaching meditation.

As the daylight began to dim, we were crossing over into Nebraska and began discussing where we might stay for the night. I generously offered my friend Mary's place, reassuring the others she'd love the company and the surprise.

At about 3 a.m. we arrived in Boulder. I directed our trusty driver Mark right up to Mary's house. Luckily, the front door was unlocked and all four of us tip-toed in with our sleeping bags beneath our arms.

About 8:00 that morning, I heard someone in the kitchen. We all woke up, of course, concerned about how Mary might react to all of us sprawled out across her living room floor. I wondered why Mary hadn't come in to see what was going on in her living room. So, I quietly approached the kitchen and peeked in. My partners in crime watched me eagerly for an affirming response. I turned my head and whispered, "It's not her. But surely she is in the other bedroom sleeping." I stepped gently, trying to hush the creaking wooden floor. I ever so carefully nudged open the bedroom door. Biting my lip, I did not want to turn around. I shook my head. "That's not her either!" I reluctantly confessed.

At that, Mark stood up inside of his sleeping bag and hopped his six-foot-two-self out of the house, down the stairs, and into the street. My two girl friends followed suit. I scurried out behind them in my PJs. We all burst out laughing. They were about to ring my neck when I defended, "This is her house! I just got a letter from her last week with this return address! I don't get it!"

They sent me back into the house to set things straight. I soon found out that, just a week prior, Mary and her roommate Marilyn had moved upstairs, switching apartments with Marilyn's brother, who, for some reason, wanted to be downstairs. So in fact, we had arrived at the correct house. We just slept in the wrong apartment.

I never heard the end of that one. To this day, some 25 years later, we tell this story to newcomers in our circle. The joke is always on me. What can I do but laugh?

One sunny day while I was studying photography and living in Los Angeles, I went window-shopping in Santa Monica. A beautiful hand-sewn quilt mesmerized me. As I pressed my face up to the glass to get a better look at it, I suddenly heard a holler. "You frickin' midget. We don't want your kind here! Get out of our town!"

I couldn't believe it. I whipped around to see who had the audacity! All I saw were three elderly ladies sitting on a bus stop bench. They looked at me in total disbelief. Wasn't them, I thought.

I glanced out to the street and saw a pink low-rider convertible. In it were two guys, both laughing their heads off. I recognized them! Mark—my "funny-man" pal from TM school (the one in the hopping sleeping bag)—stood up and waved at me. He yelled, "Hey, Peggers-now! Long time no see!"

Oh, it was a joke, I realized with relief. The sting evaporated instantly and I ran over next to the car, which had slowed down. When they came to a stop, I dove headfirst into the back seat and we zipped off.

As I ascended back to the up-right position, I peeked back behind me. The three ladies on the bus bench had fallen on the ground in disbelief. Not really. But their jaws hit the ground. I smiled and waved to them as we sped off into the sunset.

As my dad says, "It's not *what* you say, it's the *way* you say it." I guess that applies to Mark and me that day in Santa Monica. When someone pokes fun, you have to take into consideration who said it and what your relationship is. Mark's comment was extremely harsh. But then, I knew Mark was "Mr. Crude," and we had been joking about my size for years. Once, on Halloween, he dressed up as *me*! He snuck into my room and took some of my clothes. Of course, when he put them on he busted right through them! The torn foot of my tights didn't even cover his knees. He tied my shoes together and swung them over his shoulder. His long blond wig swayed across his back as he walked. "I went to bed 3 feet 8. I woke up 6 feet 2. Oh my! What a night!" he chanted as he strolled the campus in my one of a kind yellow duck skirt. So, you see, everything is relative. Mark is probably the only person alive who could have gotten away with rude remarks like that, that day in Santa Monica. That was because I knew he loved me. And he still loves me because I can laugh at myself.

So, expand! Be BIG and laugh at yourself. It's good medicine for a much too serious world.

❺

CONVEY GRATITUDE

A sure sign of inner size is the ratio between how much someone complains about what they *don't have* and how much they appreciate what they *do have*.

I recall when I was overcome with inner small-ness, I seemed to always pay attention to what I did **not** have. Mostly, I was sad because I didn't have an intimate relationship and felt slighted because of it. I'd wake up in the morning and think, "I don't want to be here. I don't want to go through another day of suffering. Enough." And begrudgingly, I would mope through my day gathering evidence on just how dreadful life really was.

Now, when I wake up, I feel an instant sense of

gratitude for being given the chance to enjoy another day of life. I feel appreciation for my excellent health, and usually take time to thank each part of my body—my vital organs, blood, bones, muscles, feet, hands, senses, and my incredible brain—for all the work they constantly do. I thank the lords of peace for granting me a place to live where there is no war. I appreciate the morning light, as well as the warmth my blanket and the walls my abode provide. I feel grateful for all the beautiful clothing hanging in my closet. I love my house and all the lovely things that fill each room. I feel awe when I step out my front door and begin taking in the magnificent variety and splendor of the natural world. I'm grateful for the people I know and don't know, and for those who guide and protect me. Every day, I'm overwhelmed with how much I can be grateful for.

Are you grateful for being alive, for your health and prosperity? How many things do you take for granted? Are you among the privileged? Can you see? Read? Walk? Think? Do you have things to be grateful for that you may have overlooked?

As you expand into your HUGE self, your attention moves away from lack and onto abundance, away from grievance and onto gratitude. Your heart opens up and you take in the wonder of the "little things" in life. Your eyes begin to see the miracles of life that surround you, and you stand in awe, in humble recognition. Your mind stops racing and you begin to just be HERE, soaking up the delight of the moment. You become a lover of life.

Here is one of my favorite passages from my teacher, the founder of the Ridhwan School and author A.H. Almaas:

> The lover is the one who is celebrating existence. The life of the lover is an ongoing love affair with the world and everything in it. You love your beloved, you love life, other people, truth, understanding—everything—sometimes with passion, sometimes with gentleness or with sweetness. You are always in love. There is no one object for your love. You embrace it all. The moment love is restricted to one person or thing, it is limited and diminished. The lover is in love with everything all the time. You look at a small white cloud, you feel dizzy. It starts raining and you are enchanted. A car goes by and you are thrilled. A lover really is mad in a sense. She experiences no barriers, no partitions, no holding back, no doubts. A lover is someone who is completely involved in existence, completely participating, someone who is not trying to get anywhere—she's already there! The lover is someone who is just loving and enjoying what is there at every minute.
>
> -From *Diamond Heart Book Two*

Don't keep your gratitude and its immeasurable beauty to yourself. Convey it. Speak it—aloud, in prayer, in your heart, to yourself, to others. Write a thank you note, write a dozen. Express the fullness as it grows inside of you. And always cherish what you have.

EXERCISE Keep a Gratitude Journal

This is a popular exercise these days; many people including Oprah suggest it. Your Gratitude Journal is a special journal where you write daily about the things you are grateful for. When you sit down to write, skim your day in your mind. Jot down the things you feel appreciation for, the "little things," blessings or special moments. You can write about a child, a friend, or an unexpected encounter when you were touched in a significant way. Write about things you are happy for, things you feel thankful for, about yourself, your family, your home, your friends, your body, life, world, whatever. This daily practice helps to build inner BIGness. The more you place your attention on the gifts in your life, the more content and peaceful you will be.

❻

BE POWERFUL
YET KIND

Many people think it is possible to be powerful OR it is possible to be kind, but not both simultaneously. Many say these two energies contradict one another.

Some leaders have embodied both power and kindness. Mahatma Gandhi is a prime example; Christ is another; Mother Teresa another; and many saints. Power combined with kindness requires a high level of conscious awareness and a great amount of inner BIGness.

Our culture makes a distinct separation between these human capacities and each is designated to a specific gender. Men are thought to be power-

> "
> *With courage you will dare to take risks, have the strength to be compassionate and the wisdom to be humble. Courage is the foundation of integrity.*
> "
>
> —KESHAVAN NAIR

ful, strong, aggressive, and warrior-like. Women are regarded as kind, gentle, nourishing and loving. Many people assume these qualities are inherent in each gender.

Folks in the personal growth and psychological arenas often talk about the need to integrate and balance these energies. "Men must get in touch with their feminine side, and women with their male side if there is to be hope for our race," they say.

The truth is, every single human being is naturally powerful AND naturally gentle. Which of these two qualities—power or kindness—is stronger in us stems from the behaviors that were encouraged by others as we grew up. No male is incapable of tenderness. Likewise, no female is powerless. We all have equal access because both of these qualities are inherent in every human being.

As we expand inside, we begin to grow BOTH of these capacities. As we come to know our True Self, we gain access to our essential nature, which is both powerful and gentle. So it is not a gender thing; it is what happens when we become whole.

Be powerful yet kind. Lead with loving kindness. Direct with compassion. Rule with care for all. These are the qualities of people who are BIG inside, people who truly WALK TALL.

BE PRESENT

"
*Think
contentment your
greatest wealth*
"

—GEORGE SHELLEY

Being present means experiencing what is happening in this moment as fully as possible. We can perceive the present moment on many levels— physically, mentally, emotionally, energetically, and spiritually. So being present can enrich our experience on all these levels in any given moment.

As our ability to be present increases, we expand our capacity to take in what life offers us in deeper, more complete ways. Receiving what's happening in the moment is how we become fulfilled, how we become content.

Author Wayne Dyer says, "We are not human beings having a spiritual experience. We are spiritual beings having a human experience." It is through the conduit of presence (or being present) that we understand ourselves as spiritual beings. It is then that our experiences generate gratitude for God and the creation. It is then that God has greater glory.

The gifts of presence are many. Presence brings about clarity of mind and the ability to focus. We are able to take in many details on many levels about what's happening. These details help us be objective. When we can assess what's really happening, we are better able to know what needs to be done next and respond most appropriately. Our memory is greatly enhanced from presence, and it allows us to better hear our inner guidance.

When we can be present with the people we love, they feel honored. They get the message they are important to us, thus love grows. Presence supports us connecting with others in a real way. Love flows in present time. Presence allows us to be available to take in big, exciting, bang-over-the-head kinds of things in life. It also lets us be open to receive the blessings delivered in less obvious ways. We're nourished by the "little" things like the sweetness of a flower, the delight of gazing into someone's eyes, the warmth of a breeze splashing across our faces, the taste of a ripe strawberry. These little things give life its splendor and nourish our souls.

One evening I was having dinner with a friend at an outdoor restaurant. I had had a particularly difficult day, and had focused on remaining present through all of it, including a trying session with Morton. When I sat down in the restaurant and looked around, something in my percept-

ability had shifted significantly. The people sitting and eating around me no longer appeared separate from me. The particulars that usually divide us—things such as age, race, gender, and style—faded into the background. What was undeniably prominent was the sense of being One, that we were all connected in some subtle yet powerful way. I not only felt it; I could also see it. Every person appeared completely precious and beautiful, even the guy next to me smoking a cigarette. A veil had been pulled back and I could see more clearly, more objectively. Presence washed the windows of my perception and gave me a most astounding gift.

Presence can get blocked when we get caught up (mentally and/or emotionally) in the past or future. When we are worried or afraid, our ability to be present gets obscured. Sometimes it's difficult to stay with what is happening because it is painful, unpleasant, or too intense. When we're on the prowl for our next "high"—the next great experience, the next fabulous person to meet, the next outrageous thing to have—we push aside the present moment as if it were not good enough. Even though staying present is not easy, it liberates us from the exhaustion, boredom, or emptiness of superficial living.

To be present, focus on what is taking place in and around you. Take a deep breath. Become aware of your arms and legs. Sense your heart. Allow it to open. Let go of worry and mental chatter. Silence that inner critical voice. Slow down when you eat, when you speak, when you walk through the garden, when you hang out with your kids, or take time to yourself.

Just slow down and settle in. Let the wonder of the moment seep into you like warm sunshine. Allow yourself to "stop" throughout your day to take in all the wonders life is giving to you. Be nourished by the little things; take in the grand things with gusto. Be here now—fully—and ENJOY!

As they say, "This moment is the greatest gift you can receive. That's why they call it the present!"

8

REVEL
IN INTIMACY

As presence grows, we develop the capacity for intimacy, which is the ability to connect deeply. Most of us have experienced intimacy in romantic love and know how lovely it is.

As the writing from Almaas in the previous chapter suggests, "the lover of life" is not restricted to loving only one or a few people, but in feeling that intimate connection with all of life. The delight of intimacy can expand outside the confines of romantic love or sexual connection. It can enrich our relationships with everyone and everything. We can enjoy intimacy with ourself, our partner, our children, even our pets, family members, and associates.

Our hearts and souls long for intimacy, the elixir of life. It is the glue of relationships. It gives us the ability to hold our relationships together when stress, differences, and conflict pull us in opposing ways.

Our modern culture itself pulls our attention in many directions. Indeed, it advocates superficial awareness and separation. Many interests around us often distract us from being in the present moment. Thus we are robbed of the delight of intimacy. Many fear being hurt, being exposed, and becoming vulnerable from loving deeply. Many fear union itself.

We must be BIG, brave, and courageous to open ourselves up to others and to live in a deep way. We must trust that adage, "to have loved and lost is better than to never have loved at all." We must allow our heart to long for what it wants—deep connection—and to open up to it.

So start to invite more depth in your relationships—with yourself, your family members, friends, your surroundings, with all of life. Develop your inner life and a deep connection with your Self. That is the ground on which all intimacy can then build. Practice being present. Open yourself to feel your life. Allow love to flow between yourself and others. Don't hold it in. Let it gush forth like a river. Take time to just "be" with your beloved, yourself, your children. If necessary, schedule time to do "nothing." Turn off the TV, video, DVD. Put your book down. Instead of focusing on things, focus on people. Look at them intently. Allow eye contact. Invite people into your heart. Let them gaze into your heart of hearts. Share your secret dreams and aspirations. Let yourself show up in a "new" way altogether.

For couples wanting deeper intimacy, I suggest studying Tantra Yoga. This discipline offers innumerable techniques for growing closer and enjoying sexual, emotional, and spiritual intimacy. *(See Muir, Charles and Caroline. **The Art of Conscious Loving** in the Reading List.)*

The enchantment of intimacy can fill your every moment. It does not have to be restricted to romantic relationships. We can enjoy intimacy with whomever we are with, including ourselves.

So open your heart. Let the grace of love thrill your self, enrich your life, and nourish your soul. Allow love, deep love, wherever you go and you will be WALKING TALL.

9

ASK YOURSELF THE BIG QUESTION:

"WHAT WOULD LOVE DO NOW?"

Asking the "big question"—*What would love do now?*—brings us to our highest sensibilities. It implies, "How can I best support, assist, help, and evolve this situation?" Not with force and dominance, but with gentle power, with intelligent compassion, and with the power of love.

"
We can do no great things—only small things with great love.
"

—KATHERINE MANSFIELD

People who ask this question know they are connected to all of existence. They see no separation between themselves and others in the "big picture." They know that what they do to others, they do to themselves.

Asking this question takes us from our minds to our hearts, from being a separate entity to being a part of humanity, from being someone who is out for oneself to someone who cares about others. This shows movement from inner smallness to inner BIGness.

> "
> There is hunger for ordinary bread, and there is hunger for love, for kindness, for thoughtfulness, and this is the greatest poverty that makes people suffer so much.
> "
>
> —MOTHER TERESA

The "big question" is what people who are BIG inside ask themselves. They ask it any time of the day—when they walk down the street, give a report to a boss, work out differences with a teenager, or have a conversation with a friend.

When you are upset and find yourself getting pushy, impatient, or mean, ask yourself: *What would love do now?* Check in for an answer. I bet it differs from what your prior inclination might have been. Think of the last argument or heated discussion you had. Might it have gone differently had you asked the "big question" half way into it?

How might your relationships be different if you asked this question several times during the day? What if you were to make your decisions or adjust your attitude toward yourself from that place of love?

You embody a giant heart and soul when you ask the "big question." So let yourself really act according to the highest ideals. Outgrow your urge to criticize, dominate, seek revenge, or show concern only about yourself.

Be HUGE! Let your interest for the betterment of all embrace everything you do, say, and feel. This is WALKING TALL.

10

SENSE YOUR CONNECTION TO ALL THAT IS

In the beginning, as a baby, you grew and learned how to function in the world. As an adult, you continue your growth on the inside. You expand your sense of self by connecting with your spirit. You learn how to love better and how to lead from your heart. As your heart heals from past traumas, you begin to enjoy life in a whole new way: from a delicate sense of beauty, wonder, and sweetness. You embrace its essence more and more; you feel an intimate connection with everything and everyone. This is the path of WALKING TALL.

What a remarkable phenomenon when we begin to see predominately with our hearts. As the heart blossoms, so does our capacity for being present and feeling intimately connected with everybody. Our hearts become happier as they expand. We feel love and gratitude for everything. We are able to accept and enjoy increasingly more aspects of ourselves and of life itself.

With a whole and healthy heart, we begin to see we are not separate from God, others, or creation. Somehow, mysteriously, we do not begin and end with the confines of our skin. We perceive we are actually made of the same substance as all of creation. Our subtle senses let us know that something intimately in us is also in everything else. Some call it love, others consciousness, others God. Whatever name you use, know that this particular perception of the heart is the truth that sets you free—free from anguish, self-doubt, anxiety, loneliness, and fear.

Sense your heart. Sit quietly and focus on that place, allowing yourself to go deeper into it. When you walk around, allow your heart to be open and powerful. Accept what is as it is. Appreciate everything. Enjoy everyone!

These practices allow you to recognize that you are a part of everything and everything is a part

"

A human being is part of the whole, called by us 'Universe'; a part limited in time and space. He experiences himself, his thoughts, and feelings as something separated from the rest—a kind of optical delusion of his consciousness. This delusion is a kind of prison for us, restricting us to our personal desires and to affection for a few persons nearest to us.

Our task must be to free ourselves from this prison by widening our circle of compassion to embrace all living creatures, and the whole of nature in its beauty.

"

—ALBERT EINSTEIN

of you. As your sense of self expands, you feel connected with all that is. Nothing is more satisfying, more rewarding, than this.

So when your healing transforms many aspects of your experience and your life is "working," don't stop your growth there. Continue to open inside! Let your heart and soul unfold to their fullest potential. Let your sense of self expand until it recognizes the BIG truth—that you are connected to everything!

Go and be BIG, be HUGE, and express the truth of love as you WALK TALL through your life!

PART FIVE
CONCLUSION

We come to planet earth for three reasons:
1. To recognize the truth
2. To express this truth
3. To enjoy

The truth is, as Marianne Williamson wrote, you are magnificent, fabulous, and deeply connected to all that is—not a small, separate entity. The difference is in how you see yourself—either from the surface or from depth.

Look at yourself from depth and see the whole "you"—body, mind, personality, emotions, and spirit.

You may observe surface limitations or flaws. But when you perceive the diamond within you—your spirit— you see that your unlimited goodness, strength, wisdom, preciousness, and beauty are more substantial than what is on the surface.

Once you recognize the truth of your whole self, two things happen. First, your wounds begin to heal and everything in your life gets better. Second, you now have a duty to celebrate your uniqueness by expressing the truth of who you are in your daily life.

When you express that truth, you do BIG things—like spread joy, take risks, and go for what you want. You are BIG enough to laugh at yourself and express your gratitude to God, yourself, and others, even for the little things. You are powerful, yet kind. You are deeply present in each moment and thus enjoy an intimate connection with all of life. You come from your heart, knowing you are a part of the whole, never alone, never unloved. Your sense of self expands beyond the walls of your skin and you see what only the heart can see: that you are made of the same substance as all that is.

> "
> One in All,
> All in One—
> If only this is
> realized, No more
> worry about your
> not being perfect!
> "
>
> —SENG-TS'AN

You are one with everything. Your life is a celebration, and everything and everyone in it a gift. This is the life of inner BIGness. This is WALKING TALL!

So, fulfill your purpose. Recognize the truth of "you." Express that in each moment each day. And while all that is happening, always ENJOY!

family Christmas, 1997

at camp,
age 6

age 13 with the "fam"

age 12 with the real
"Rin-Tin-Tin"

O'Neill Girl-Power, 1990

With a butterfly too!

Mom and Dad

Beautiful
Colorado,
'997

Merry
Christmas
from us
to you

First date with Brad and LP friends

Someone from my planet

On the platform,
2000

Walking Tall

Skiing,
1995

A dream come true,
a custom kitchen

adapting

adapting

There's just so much to say…

FREQUENTLY ASKED QUESTIONS ABOUT LITTLE PEOPLE:

- **Is there a particular height that distinguishes an average-sized person from a short-statured person?**

    According to Little People of America, an adult who stands 4 feet 10 inches or shorter is considered to be a Little Person (LP).

- **When I meet or talk to someone of short stature, do they prefer I stand up or squat down?**

    Most people like to have face-to-face contact when they are conversing. If you greet a Little Person briefly, it seems fine to remain standing. If you are going to get into a conversation, sitting down, putting one knee down, or squatting would allow better face-to-face contact and make both parties feel more comfortable.

- **What is the politically correct term for someone who is very short?**

    Most people who are very short prefer to be called "a person of short stature" or "a Little Person." The terms midget and dwarf are reserved for conversations concerning medical issues. Otherwise, those terms can be offensive.

- **What's the difference between a midget and a dwarf?**

    Medically speaking, midgets are individuals with short stature whose limbs are similar in proportion to those of average-sized people. Midgets can go into a children's clothing store, buy an outfit, and wear it that evening. Dwarves, on the other hand, must have the majority of their clothing altered to fit or custom made. Dwarves are distinguished by their short limbs. Their arms and legs are shorter in proportion to their body size compared to those same proportions in an average-sized person.

- **What is the most common type of dwarfism?**

  About 80% of all Little People are diagnosed with a type of short stature called acondroplasia. The distinguishing features of a person with acondroplasia are a large head with short arms and legs. Commonly, the third and fourth fingers bend in opposite directions.

  The other 20% of Little People have one variety of more than 150 types of dwarfism. My type of dwarfism falls in this category and its official name is acromesomelia.

- **Can average-sized parents have a short-statured child?**

  Yes, most Little People are born to average-sized parents.

- **How does this happen?**

  No one really knows for sure. It's like asking why are there hundreds of breeds of dogs, types of flowers, or kinds of trees. Nature has a built-in mechanism that creates and supports variation and diversity.

  This mechanism in genetic science is known as genetic mutation. Mutations of any sort are deviations from the norm. In dwarves, a variation occurs in the genetic blueprint that oversees bone growth. The blueprint tells the living organism, "your bone growth will be different than it is for most people."

- **How often does dwarfism occur?**

  For average-sized parents of children with acondroplasia,

the chances are about one in 40,000.

For average-sized parents of children with the more uncommon types of dwarfism, the chances are much less, anywhere from one in a million to one in a billion.

- ## Can Little People have children?

Yes. Even though Little People don't grow as tall as average-sized people, they mature just the same in all other ways. They grow up to have the same aspirations, desires, needs, and problems as average-sized people. Most people, tall or small, want to experience romantic love, to make a good living contributing to society, and aspire to becoming a parent. Many adult Little People enjoy both the thrill and challenges of parenthood.

- ## If a Little Person has a baby, will it be average in size or short-statured?

The answer is very complex because most Little People carry dominant genes, but some LPs carry recessive genes. In each combination the probable outcomes differ.

With two LP parents carrying a dominant gene (such as for acondroplasia) there is a 50% chance of having a short-statured child, a 25% chance of having an average-sized child, and a 25% chance of the child getting a "double dose" of the dominant gene, which is not conducive to life.

When the LP carries a recessive gene, it has to match up with the exact same gene to be expressed. If the LP with a recessive gene marries an average-sized person, their children will be carriers of the recessive gene, but the child will grow to average size. If a person with a recessive gene (like me) has a baby with an LP with a dominant gene, (like Brad) they have a 50/50 chance of having a baby with the dominant type of dwarfism. So, Brad and I have a 50/50 chance of having a baby whose stature characteristics would resemble the traits of Brad (who has a very rare type of dwarfism call Tattoo-syndrome). If the child didn't get Brad's dominant gene, it would grow to average size but inherit a recessive gene from me.

With a mixed couple, (one short-statured parent with a dominant gene and one average-sized parent) their chances of having a short-statured child are 50/50.

That's a lot of mathematical mumbo-jumbo. If you don't quite understand it, that's okay. The important point is that differences are the glory of this creation.

- **How can parents tell if their baby is a Little Person?**

Many times in the first three years, it is difficult to tell. Because acondroplasia is the most common type of dwarfism, many doctors and pediatricians are familiar with its distinguishing features in infants such as a large head and short arms. With other types of dwarfism, the distinctive features often do not usually become apparent until the child is a toddler. If you notice your child has short arms and legs, a lack of agility or ease in walking, stiffness in joints, or of course, shortness in height, you might seek the advise of a specialist in short stature at the John Hopkins Hospital in Maryland.

- **Are there any organizations for Little People?**

There is an organization called Little People of America. LPA was founded in 1957 by a short-statured actor named Billy Barty. The first meeting had 20 attendees. Between then and now, the organization has grown to more than 7,300 members.

Little People of America is a national organization. It holds local and regional chapter meetings, medical symposiums, and social get-togethers. Every summer, a national convention takes place in a different U.S. city. LPA members gather to compete athletically, attend workshops, have lots of fun, and dance eye-to-eye. Many doctors with a specialty in short stature attend the conferences as well. They hold panel discussions and meet with parents, discussing their child's specific needs.

For more information about LPA, visit its web site at: www.LPAonline.org. Or you can call the LPA Hotline at 1-888-LPA-2001. The LPA web site provides information from the medical field as well as books and references for those wanting more information about LPs. It also features a chat room.

- **Where can I find adaptations for Little People?**

    The LPA web site offers lots of information on: adaptations for reaching light switches, portable stools, automobile pedal extensions, and more.

- **Is it possible to adopt children with short stature?**

    Yes. If you go to the LPA web site, call the LPA hotline, or subscribe to the LPA newsletter, you can obtain the current opportunities for adopting a child of short stature.

Suggested Resource List

Anna Halprin's Tamalpa Institute
PO Box 794
Kentfield, CA 94914
Phone: 415-457-8555
Web site: www.tamalpa.org

Hakomi Somatics Institute
PO Box 19438
Boulder, CO 80308
Phone: 303-447-3290
Web site: www.hakomisomatics.com

The Ridhwan Foundation
aka The Diamond Heart and Training Institute
PO Box 2747
Berkeley, CA 94702
Phone: 510-841-1283
Web site: www.ridhwan.org

Transcendental Meditation (TM)
TM is taught in centers all around the world. To find a TM center
in your locale, go to www.tm.org or look in the phone book under
"Transcendental Meditation."

Little People of America (LPA)
LPA Hotline: 1-888-LPA-2001
Web site: www.LPAonline.org.

National Speakers Association
1500 South Priest Drive
Tempe, AZ 85281
Phone: 480-968-2552
Web site: www.nsaspeaker.org

Eeo Stubblefield Photography
E-mail: eeos@ulster.net

Suggested Reading List

Almaas, A.H. *Diamond Heart, Book One: Elements of the Real in Man.* Denver, CO: Shamabala Publications, 2000.

Almaas, A.H. *Essence With the Elixir of Enlightenment.* Denver, CO: Samuel Weiser, 1998.

Almaas, A.H. *The Pearl Beyond Price: Integration of Personality into Being...* Denver, CO: Shamabala Publications, 2000.

Balch, James and Phyllis. *Prescription for Nutritional Healing: A Practical A-Z Reference to Drug-Free Remedies.* New York: Avery, 2000.

Binaet, Calla Marie. *Tears Flow, Ice Melts, Spring Comes!* Boulder, CO: Golden Reed, 1997.

Campbell, Anthony. *Seven States of Consciousness: A Vision of Possibilities.* New York: Harper & Row, 1974.

Campbell, Eileen, editor. *A Dancing Star: Inspirations to Guide and Heal.* San Francisco: Harper Collins, 1995.

Chopra, Deepak, M.D. *Ageless Body, Timeless Mind: The Quantum Alternative to Growing Old.* New York: Three Rivers Press, 1998.

Duffy, William, F. *Sugar Blues.* New York: Warner Books, 1993.

Flick, Deborah L., Ph.D. *From Debate to Dialogue: Using the Understanding Process to Transform Our Conversations.* Boulder, CO: Orchid Publications, 1998.

Francina, Suza. *The New Yoga For People Over Fifty: A Comprehensive Guide For Midlife and Older Beginners.* Deerfield Beach, Florida: Health Communications Inc., 1997.

Gendlin, Eugene, Ph.D. *Focusing.* New York: Bantam Books Inc., 1982.

Kundtz, Dr. David. *Everyday Serenity: Meditations for People Who Do Too Much.* Berkeley, CA: Conari Press, 2000.

Kundtz, Dr. David. *Stopping: How to Be Still When You Have to Keep Going.* Berkeley, CA: Conari Press, 1998.

Kurtz, Ron. *Body-Centered Psychotherapy: The Hakomi Method.* Mendocino, CA: LifeRhythm, 1997.

Maupin, Armistead. *Maybe the Moon.* New York: Harper Collins, 1993.

Millman, Dan. *Way of the Peaceful Warrior: A Book That Changes Lives.* H J Kramer, 2000.

Mitchell, W. *It's Not What Happens To You, It's What You Do About It.* Arvada, CO: Phoenix Press, 2001.

Muir, Charles and Caroline. *Tantra: The Art of Conscious Loving.* San Francisco, CA: Mercury House, 1989.

Peck, M. Scott. *The Road Less Traveled: A New Psychology of Love.* New York: Touchstone, 1998.

Stern-LaRosa, Caryl, Ellen Hofheimer Bettmann. *Hate Hurts: How Children Learn and Unlearn Prejudice.* New York: Scholastic Inc., 2000.

Wilbur, Ken. *A Brief History of Everything.* Boston, MA: Shambhala Publications Inc., 2001.

Winget, Larry. *The Simple Way to Success.* Tulsa, Oklahoma: Win Publications!, 2000.

Yogi, Maharishi Mahesh. *Science of Being and Art of Living: Transcendental Meditation.* New York: Meridan Books, 1994.

ABOUT THE AUTHOR

PEGGY O'NEILL stands 3 feet 8 inches tall. Tiny in stature and HUGE in presence, Peggy delivers a far-reaching message: "WALK TALL! Honor yourself, accept others, and express your inherent magnificence. Everyone can be BIG on the INside."

For much of her life, Peggy felt diminished by physical limitation and social prejudice. Triumphing over many difficulties, she now possesses confidence, resiliency, compassion, and wisdom. Today, she radiates these qualities in her work to inspire and lead others toward success and happiness.

As an author, inspirational speaker, diversity trainer, and life-coach, Ms. O'Neill enchants audiences of all ages from all walks of life. Peggy is a certified Hakomi psychotherapist and has earned a degree in Education from MIU and a degree in Commercial Photography from the Art Center College of Design.

Peggy's passion lies in the area of teaching. She conducts keynote speeches, seminars, and workshops for adults, and presents programs on celebrating diversity to children and teens.

Peggy and her husband Brad Laise, also a "Little Person," live near Santa Barbara, California, with their dogs Keesha and Wickie. If you'd like Peggy to present a keynote speech or workshop to your organization, or give a program at your elementary school assembly or teen leadership conference, just holler "Yo Peggy!"

SMALL MIRACLES UNLIMITED
P.O. Box 269 • Ojai, CA 93024
Toll free: 1-877-Yo-Peggy
E-mail: Yopeggy@aol.com
Web Site: www.yopeggy.com

ORDER FORM

Order on line at www.yopeggy.com

	PRICE	QUANTITY	TOTAL
BOOKS:			
• *Walking Tall*	$17.00	_____	$_____
Overcoming Inner Smallness, No Matter What Size You Are			
• *Little Squarehead*	$15.95	_____	$_____

color illustrated hardback...
Little Squarehead is the story of a young girl who overcomes the challenge of being different by discovering her true self. This delightfully illustrated book will inspire children of all ages to face life's challenges and to celebrate their own uniqueness.

WALKING TALL HATS
(One size, adjustable)

	PRICE	QUANTITY	TOTAL
• Periwinkle hat	$12.00	_____	$_____
• Khaki hat	$12.00	_____	$_____
• Khaki hat with charcoal bill	$12.00	_____	$_____
• Khaki hat with blue bill	$12.00	_____	$_____

WALKING TALL T-SHIRTS:
Small (S), Medium (M), Large (L), X-large (XL)

		PRICE	QUANTITY	TOTAL
• Yellow	Size _____	$15.00	_____	$_____
• Periwinkle	Size _____	$15.00	_____	$_____
• Gray	Size _____	$15.00	_____	$_____

AUDIO TAPES:

	PRICE	QUANTITY	TOTAL
• **Walking Tall Keynote**	$7.00	_____	$_____
• **Shipping and handling**	$4.00		$ 4.00
($2 for each additional book or item)			$_____

Grand Total:
$_____

Make checks payable to: Peggy O'Neill
Mail to: PO Box 269 • Ojai, CA 93024
Fax to: 1-805-640-7375

Credit card # _____ expiration date _____

NOTES

NOTES

NOTES

NOTES